D1231156

MIND PROBE - HYPNOSIS

IRENE HICKMAN, D.O.

Published by
Hickman Systems
4 Woodland Lane
Kirksville, MO 63501 U.S.A.
(816) 665-1836

ISBN 0-915689-00-6 Paperback
ISBN 0-915689-01-4 Hardback

Irene Hickman, D.O.

FOREWORD

My degree is Doctor of Osteopathy, D.O. I was trained as an Osteopathic Physician in all of the modalities taught in the allopathic or M.D. schools, but also something more. The basic philosophy that the human body is a unit and operates as an integrated whole organism was the first principle of my training. I was taught and fully accepted the premise that man must be comprehended and treated as a unit. The lesson material was interesting and I studied eagerly and well, maintaining a grade standing always in the upper twenty percent of my class. After graduation, I felt well equipped to present myself to my community as a physician and to take the responsibility for the health care of all who might seek my aid. I expected to be able to help my patients resolve their health problems with the therapies taught me in medical school.

It soon became evident that only a few could be so helped. The majority of patients who came to me continued to be ill, tense, worried or unhappy in spite of my best efforts.

New and different ways of treating them had to be found. It was clear that tranquilizers were not a permanent or even a long range solution to their problems. I acquired training in hypnosis and began using this tool with selected patients. Many who had failed to respond to former treatments now became well.

In addition, these patients began to teach me much more about the function of the human mind than I had been able to learn from other sources. By using non-directive techniques—asking questions rather than giving suggestions—I learned that there are surprising depths that could be probed. My patients taught me that at a deeper level of their consciousness there is a source of knowledge and understanding, not only as to the nature of their problems, but also the causes of each problem and the needed remedy.

During the more than thirty years of using hypnosis nondirectively for therapy, I have become completely convinced that within the subconscious of each of us there exists a level of wisdom and insight far surpassing that available in our usual state of consciousness. I learned that with the use of hypnosis it is possible to transcend both time and space, recall and relive distant memories, some even from ancient times.

i

It is relatively easy to move back through time and to probe any event previously experienced no matter how trivial or how intense the experience. Whenever an emotionally loaded memory was revealed and the incident relived, there was a reported definite feeling of release and relief of tension, a lessening of symptoms of illness or a movement toward resolving personal relationships. My patients further taught me that more is required than just simple recall. Often it was necessary to guide the hypnotized subject to again and again relive the unpleasant incident. Each additional time allowed the release of more of the emotion. It was my custom to ask them to go through the experience enough times that the feelings were completely released—until no emotional charge was left. When the emotion was fully expended, then the malfunction of the body, mind or emotions could easily be corrected. Often there was self-correction of problems.

The ease with which most of my patients would move into light, moderate or deep states of hypnosis and respond to simple requests was continually surprising. All that was required was to allow the time for relaxation of body and mind with any one of a great variety of hypnotic induction techniques. I would then ask them to move back through time to any event, experience or happening that caused or helped to cause their problem. In most cases there was prompt compliance. The request, being non-specific, allowed the subject complete freedom to move through time a short ways to recent events, further back to childhood or infancy or even to before birth.

A high percentage of my patients related emotionally charged events from former life experiences, and would continue to be ill or troubled until these distant memories were tapped and the ancient emotions released. It was my policy to direct the patients to move back through time to find the cause of their distress. I did not specifically direct them to go back to former lives.

Dr. Lewis Thomas, Consultant to the Memorial Sloan-Kettering Cancer Center in New York, wrote a few years ago. "The solidest piece of scientific truth I know is that we are profoundly ignorant about nature. Indeed, I regard this the major discovery of the past hundred years of biology.....This sudden confrontation with the depth and scope of ignorance represents the most significant contribution of twentieth century science to the human intellect. We are, at last, facing up to it. In earlier times, we either pretended to understand how things worked or ignored the problem, or simply made up stories to fill the gaps. Now that we have begun exploring in earnest, doing serious science, we are getting glimpses of how huge the questions are, and how far they are from being answered."

It is my hope that this book will begin to answer some of the questions.

The contents of this book will be disturbing to many—particularly those who dislike the idea of prior lives—of reincarnation. I do not expect that I have written to constitute proof for those who disagree. These I challenge to repeat the work I have done and then form their own opinions. I predict that anyone who uses my methods will have the same type of results that I have had.

It is not difficult to learn to work with hypnosis. Many of the more than 200 books on the subject of hypnosis now in print are excellent aids. My favorites, particularly for beginners, are *Hypnotism Handbook*, by Cooke and Van Vogt, and *New Master Course in Hypnosis*, by Harry Arons.

Through the use of any one of a number of different induction techniques, subjects can be helped to attain as great a depth of hypnosis as they are able to reach. Then all that is required is to simply suggest that they move back through time to a past incident of importance to them, one which caused or contributed to a problem, or simply an incident the reliving of which will give them a greater understanding of themselves. In most cases the hypnotized subject will respond promptly and when requested will relate what they are experiencing.

One word of warning. Rarely (but it can happen at any time—even with the very first hypnosis) a subject will begin expressing strong emotion. This can be quite disconcerting for the inexperienced hypnotist and give a strong inclination to stop the session and waken the subject. If this is done the subject will be uncomfortable or upset or both. Such situations must be handled as follows—the subject must be allowed to express the emotion completely. I have frequently suggested that whatever feeling they are expressing, sorrow, fear, anger or any other will be fully expressed in one minute (or any other appropriate time period) and they will feel relieved. They continue to discharge emotions for the suggested period, then become quiet and calm. After calmness has returned, I would either continue the session or waken them. I do not waken them when they are in a state of high emotion.

When this plan is followed, no distress is carried into the waking time. A clue as to whether enough emotion has been released lies in the subject's feelings of comfort or discomfort upon awakening. If there is remaining discomfort, then the emotions have not been sufficiently drained or released.

Traditional hypnotherapy has used hypnosis differently. Instead of being non-directive and asking questions only, it is customary to limit the hypnotherapy sessions to the giving of suggestions. This has been beneficial in many cases. However, it does nothing to discover, reveal and dissipate old traumatic experiences that are still causing trouble.

My patients have taught me well to take the attitude always that they, the subjects, have a reliable source of inner knowledge and guidance that can be called upon. Each subject is far wiser about the many facets of himself than I could ever be.

At present my work is principally teaching others to apply this method of non-directive hypnotherapy. I emphasize to my students, "Remember that your subject knows much more about himself or herself than you will ever know. Deemphasize direct suggestions and concentrate on the exploratory question. Guide them gently in the way they want to go."

This method when followed has a minimum of danger and a maximum of benefit.

Hypnosis, though long ignored, is now coming of age and is being used more and more by the helping professionals. Hypnosis is probably the finest tool available for the probing of the human mind. Its increased use non-directively will undoubtably bring us ever closer to the answers to questions as to who, what, and why we are and to how our minds *really function.*

TABLE OF CONTENTS

Chapter 1

HAUNTED BY AN ANCIENT FEAR

*"Life is the soul's nursery—its training place for
the destinies of eternity."*   Wm. M. Thackeray

An important chapter in the history of my use of hypnosis developed in the summer of 1956. The case described here marked a turning point in my understanding and use of hypnotherapy.

B.... E.... came to me in May of 1956 with the complaint of a sense of panic that would appear suddenly and frequently. She felt this panic as a sharp pressure over her heart. When these attacks would come she would have to use the utmost self-control to avoid running screaming down the street. She had had extensive treatment from other physicians including psychiatrists over a period of several years, had been hospitalized for several months in a private mental hospital and had taken a variety of tranquilizers—all without benefit. Instead, the panic attacks were becoming more frequent and more severe. She had found that getting a little drunk would help somewhat and had reached the point that she was leaving work early almost every afternoon and drinking more and more heavily. She said she knew that this was a dead-end road she was on and asked my help.

She responded well to hypnotizeability tests and was an excellent subject—one who reached a deep state of hypnosis quickly—yet was able to speak clearly and distinctly, responding promptly without the long pauses that are common with most hypnotic subjects.

My appointment book was crowded, so I gave her an appointment for two weeks ahead.

The heavy work schedule indicated the need for an assistant. As so often happens in my life, when a need is felt, a means of filling it is promptly provided.

M...., a trained and skilled hypnotherapist, who had been trained by Charles Cooke, author of *Hypnotism Handbook*, came and asked whether she might work with me under my supervision using hypnosis. I was impressed by her skill and her sensitivity and agreed that we could work together.

I mentioned that some of my hypnotized patients regressed into former lives. She strenuously rejected this as "poppycock", but agreed that the non-directive approach was the method of choice.

M's first day on the job had no patients specifically scheduled for her. She was getting familiar with the office layout and routines and helping where she could.

B. E. came in without an appointment in a most distressed state. She had drunk more than usual the day before and was suffering a severe hangover. She was crying and moaning, shaking agitatedly and creating quite a disturbance in the waiting room.

I asked M. to take her into the front therapy room and get her quiet, saying only that she was a good subject for hypnosis and that I would join them as soon as I could. They went in together and the waiting room again became quiet and calm.

After an interval of about fifteen minutes, M. came out of the room wearing a perplexed, even frustrated expression. She showed me a note pad on which she had written 1780, Gleesbeck's, Susan McDonald, etc. I realizes that B. E. was talking about a former life. I hastily offered assurances that it was all right and that I would be with her soon. I finished quickly with the other patients and then entered the front therapy room. This is the scene that met my eyes.

Stretched out on the therapy couch, B. E. was obviously in deep hypnosis, a condition easily discerned by the trained observer. Beside her sat M. totally bewildered.

B. E. was shouting in a loud voice, "I *told* you it's April 17, 1780, and I'm dead. I'm on the floor."

Had I deliberately planned, I could not have arranged a more potent initiation for M. Her insistent rejection of the possibility of reincarnation was being inescapably challenged on her first day in my office.

I later learned that M. had suggested to B. E. once she

was hypnotized, to go back to the origin of her complaint. B. E. had gone at once to 1780, saying that her name was Susan McDonald with a husband, Johnathon, and a daughter, Annie. Johnny spent most of his time and money at Gleesbeck's tavern leaving his wife and daughter without food or fuel. He had come home in a drunken state carrying a tankard of ale. She had nagged and he had knocked her down. Her head hit the leg of the stove and she had died.

Repeatedly M. had tried to dissuade her. B. E. would not be dissuaded even by the considerable skill of M. I had entered the room just after M's third attempt to get B. E. to let the 1780 scene fade and go back to the source of her panic attacks.

Often have I wished that those three attempts at dissuasion had been recorded. Unfortunately, there had been no recorder in the room.

I rushed out, returning with a recorder and turned it on. Following is a verbatim transcript of that recording:

M.   What's happening?

B. E.   It's eighteen oh three and I'm still waiting.

M.   What are you waiting for?

B. E.   I have to come back — to work this out! That's the only reason I have to come back.

M.   You have to work out this fear?

B. E.   That's right. Everybody else is waiting too. Some go back though when they ask, and I keep asking and asking. (mimicking) 'No, not yet. No, not yet.'

M.   Now we are going forward in time to the day when you are coming back. Now tell me what day and year this is.

B. E.   It's January 19, 1932.

M.   What's happening now?

B. E.   (Very softly) Now, now, now.

M.   What's happening. Where are you?

3

B. E.   I'm in B....., North Dakota, at my mother's mother's farmhouse.

M.   What's going on?

B. E.   Well, I asked to come back.

M.   You asked to come back.

B. E.   I asked, so-o-o-o, (long pause). But it's so comfortable. (Another pause, then she raised her hands to the sides of her head and began to moan as she rolled her head back and forth as if in pain.)

M.   Are you hurting? What's happening to you? (B. E. continued to roll about and moan.) Here, let me help you. (Touching B. E.'s head soothingly.) Relax. I will take the pain away. When I count to three it will be gone. All you will have left is the memory. 1,2,3. Now tell me what is happening.

B. E.   (In frightened tones) They're pulling me out of my mother.

M.   Who is pulling you out?

B. E.   This doctor. (Quietly as if watching the scene.) He has a long gray beard and glasses.

M.   And where is he? At your mother's house?

B. E.   (Annoyed) At my mother's mother's house out on the farm.

B. E. again corrected M. (The traditional view of hypnosis postulates that the subject, being in a state of "heightened suggestibility," acts always in ways to please or obey the hypnotist. Our experience with B. E. and many others clearly demonstrated to us that hypnotized persons — at least *our* hypnotized patients continued to excercise freedom of choice and would not hesitate to correct us if we misunderstand a reply or misstate a question. Not only would B. E. correct our mistakes, but would do it with a strong note of annoyance bordering on disgust in her voice. Even after more than twenty-five years this tape remains one of my favorites not only for the way it came into being, but for its content and recording quality.)

M.	All right. How do you feel now? Are you comfortable? Where are you now?
B. E.	In her arms.
M.	Is she saying anything?
B. E.	No.
M.	Is anyone saying anything?
B. E.	The doctor says, "You have a fine baby girl, Mrs. J......"
M.	What's happening?
B. E.	I'm thinking.
M.	What are you thinking about?
B. E.	Two things. I'm thinking about how comfortable and close it feels.
M.	What else are you thinking?
B. E.	The reason I'm back is to take care of this feeling—this fear.
M.	What else are you thinking?
B. E.	I'm wondering how long it's going to take this time. Even though I can't say anything or express anything, I can still think. If it wasn't for the thinking it would be nice being a baby.
M.	Can you feel the fear now in your stomach?
B. E.	No! It's not in my stomach. It's right here. (She closed her fist over the center of her chest.)

Another correction of M. This time her voice showed annoyance and almost anger at M's error.

M.	Right there in your chest?
B. E.	Yes. (After a short pause she began to laugh merrily.)

M.   What's so funny?

B. E.   My grandmother brought me a bottle.

M.   What is so funny about that?

B. E.   (Very amused.) I'm thinking about how I never did like warm's cow's milk, and here it is. And there isn't anything I can do about it. I should complain. I was so hungry before. (The expression on her face changed rapidly first to serious thoughtfulness and then to fear.)

M.   What's happening now? How old are you?

B. E.   Three. (Then becoming very distressed) I forgot! I forgot those things!

M.   What did you forget?

B. E.   I forgot how to think — how to remember! Suddenly it was there, and now it isn't.

M.   We'll go back and find it. What was there? What are you looking for?

B. E.   (Speaking very softly.) God.

M.   What are you doing?

B. E.   (Puzzled.) Suddenly I can't remember.

M.   What's happening around you?

B. E.   My father is drinking. Yes, and my mother's nagging. And he picked my brother and me up and he threw us as hard as he could on the couch — no, not a couch — a leather davenport. That's when I stopped remembering. Because then I was . . . before then I was thinking. You know what I was thinking?

M.   What were you thinking?

B. E.   I was thinking, here we go all over again, the same thing. Only now my father is drinking and my mother is nagging.

M.   And before?

6

B. E.   Before, *I* nagged and Johnny drank. (Without specific directions B. E. began relating events in her present life with similar events from a former life.)

M.   Was this when you were Susan?

B. E.   But I could remember it all up until I was three.

M.   Tell me once more your name and the year you were Susan.

B. E.   Susan McDonald. 1780, April seventeen.

M.   What is your name now?

B. E.   B.... E.....

M.   All right, B......, you are three years old, and your father has thrown you on the couch, and you find you can no longer remember. All right, we will go to the next experience you do remember. I'll count to three and you will be there. 1,2,3. Tell me what's happening now and how old you are.

B. E.   I'm five and a half. I'm coming home from kindergarten. It's eight long blocks, and I have to wee-wee, and I don't know if I am going to be able to hold it or not until I get home. (Pause.) I hold it and run all the way home. I just get there in the hotel lobby. One of the men that lived there stopped and patted me on the head and said, "How's my little girl, B......?" And I wet all over the floor—because my mother told me to be polite. (Laughing.) I just couldn't hold it another minute.

M.   How did you feel about this?

B. E.   Terribly ashamed, and terribly embarassed. But if mother hadn't said to always be polite to the people in the hotel I would have just said, "Pardon me, I have to go." And he could have patted me on the head some other time.

M.   You don't have to be ashamed of this now. You

were just a little girl. Do you feel any shame about this now?

B. E.   No, I don't

M.   Is there something else you need to talk about today?

B. E.   Yes. I'm six years old.

M.   All right. You are six. Where are you? What's happening?

B. E.   We're at home and (deep sigh) my brother and I are ill. We have pneumonia.

M.   Tell me about it.

B. E.   My mother and father are arguing and she said she was going to leave him. And he said, "Well, if you are, you're not going to take the kids with you." And she said, "Oh yes I am." And then she picked us up and took us over to the Lacey's. They lived in a big white house. And he came over there and he was drunk and he chased her around the vacant lot next to their house and he kicked her. Blood just poured out of her. Just because she wouldn't go home with him.

M.   What are you doing?

B. E.   Watching out the window. Watching him kick her.

M.   How does this make you feel?

B. E.   (Sobbing) Terrible, terrible! (Screaming) Leave her alone! Oh, Mommy, Mommy. Don't kill her. Don't kill her! (She cried uncontrollably for a few minutes and then grew quiet.)

M.   Do you feel the fear?

B. E.   Oh yes, yes!

M.   Now the fear will disappear as I count to three. This happened a long time ago. You don't have to feel the fear now. 1,2,3. It's gone now. This

8

fear is gone. What else is happening? Is he still hurting her?

(Even though B. E. was told that the fear was gone, this was not effective. We had not yet found and eliminated the prime cause of the fear. Until that was done much fear remained.)

B. E.   No. She's in the house and he came in the front door and he took a bottle of Lysol out of his pocket and he said, "Doris, I'm sorry I kicked you. Get the kids and let's go home." And she said, "No." He said, "If you don't, I will drink this." And she said, "I cannot go back with you, Butler." So he drank it.

M.   Did you see him drink it?

B. E.   He drank it in the living room.

M.   Then what happened?

B. E.   Mrs. Lacey and Mom . . . Mrs. Lacey called someone and Mom tried to pour raw eggs down his throat.

M.   Where are you?

B. E.   On the Davenport.

M.   And you see this?

B. E.   Yes.

M.   How do you feel about this?

B. E.   My daddy! He's frothing all over — white foamy stuff.

M.   What are you feeling now?

B. E.   Fear. I'm so unhappy, so unhappy. (Sobbing.)

M.   All right, feel the fear, and then let it fade away. It's all gone now. What happened next?

B. E.   Some policemen come in. They looked at him and then one of them said, "It's too late."

M.   How do you feel about this?

B. E.   Very sad because my Daddy's gone. I did love him.

M.   All right, feel the sadness, and then let this feeling drift away with the other feelings. What are they doing with your father now?

B. E.   They took him out. Grandma took us over to her house.

M.   What are you doing there?

B. E.   (With intense displeasure.) Praying. Always praying!

M.   How do you feel about this?

B. E.   I don't like it. It shouldn't be that way.

M.   Tell me why you don't like it.

B. E.   Because she says that my mother killed him. Over and over, all the time we were there. (Mockingly.) "Your mother killed my son. Your mother killed my son." Drummed it in and drummed it in. Every time we would sit down at a meal there'd be some little verse from the Bible. "Read that verse. Poor children — what will become of you now?" I didn't believe that my mother killed him. I knew she didn't. I saw it.

M.   How do you feel about her saying this?

B. E.   I feel fear, because I don't know what to believe.

M.   Did you want to say or do anything about this?

B. E.   I did. I said, "My Mommy didn't kill Daddy."

M.   What did she say?

B. E.   (Sternly.) "She killed my son." I know it isn't true, but she is an adult, supposedly, and she goes to church every Sunday, and talks about everybody else. But it's all right as long as you go to church, and read your damn little Bible

10

verses before you eat. (Angry shouting.) Old hypocritical bitch!

M.   You don't like her, do you?

B. E.   No. I despise her! (Bitterly.) I hate her!

M.   All right, feel the hate and then let it fade, for you don't have to feel the hate now. This happened a long time ago. So you can let go of the hate and of any fear you feel. (After a short pause she relaxed and became calm again.) Are you still with your grandmother?

B. E.   Not the same. Mother took us out to her mother's for a while. Then I can remember some things. (Her voice became faint—almost a whisper.)

M.   Are you tired? Do you want to come back to the present time?

B. E.   Yes.

M.   All right, come back to the present time and place. You will waken feeling better than you have for a long time. You may remember some of the things we have been talking about, but nothing will disturb or alarm you. Return now to the present—June, 1956. (Pause.) You have now returned to the present. Now awaken as I count from ten to one. At the count of one you will be awake and you will feel fine. 10,9,8,7,6,5,4,3,2,1. Awake!

B. E.   (Opening her eyes slowly and smiling.) I feel so much better. Thanks.

M.   Is the fear gone?

B. E.   A lot of it. I feel so good. There is still some fear left though.

It would be easy—even tempting to attribute all of B. E.'s emotional disturbances to her tragic childhood filled with violence, parental conflict, drunkenness, father's suicide in front of her, and grandmother's accusations.

I must agree that these experiences must have contributed to her fear and insecurity. However, I wanted to reexamine her to determine with a greater certainty *all* of the contributing factors. The second session transcript (which was made the following day) begins in Chapter 2. For this session, I acted as hypnotist.

The reader will note the gentle guiding of my directions to her. This left her free to choose her responses totally without pressure from me.

After each event was related I would ask her if the fear was gone. Her negative replies were followed by my request that she go back through the incident once more. Each repetition would bring out successively diminishing intensiy of emotion.

When in this case and others the patient would tell me that the fear (or any other emotion we were working on), is gone — has been totally released — then that problem would disappear. And it would not recur.

Chapter 2

TWO MORE LIVES OF VIOLENCE

*"My opinion is that we shall be reincarnated . . .
and that hereafter we shall suffer or benefit in
accordance with what we have done in this world."*
David Lloyd George

The next day B. E. was waiting a little impatiently for
her appointment. She was anxious to search further for the
basis of her fear. M. and I arranged our schedules so that we
could both sit in with her.

She was hypnotized quickly. I said to her, "Just relax.
Your subconscious mind knows why you are afraid. Search
through your memory record for any scene which will show
you why you are afraid. You will find it and you will know it
when you do."

We waited watching a variety of expressions play over
her face for several minutes. Then an expression of puzzlement was followed by one of intense interest. At this point I
was sure that she had found a significant memory.

This is the transcript of the second session:

Dr. H. What is your name?

B. E.   (Very softly) Sahri.

Dr. H. (I had not understood her word.) Tell me your
        name.

B. E.   Sahri. (Spelling) S A H R I.

Dr. H. Sahri? (She nods) Look around you there and
        describe what you see. What's happening?

B. E.   It's in a tent on the desert.

Dr. H. Now I am a friend and I can talk with you and

you can hear me and I can hear you, but I cannot see what you see. So you will have to describe all that you see as it happens. Tell me what is happening now.

B. E.   There are beautiful, beautiful rugs and he's sitting there.

Dr. H.   Would you tell me who he is?

B. E.   (Disgustedly) Fat! He's sitting with his legs crossed and arms folded. He has something on his head. (Eyes squinted to see.) And he has white . . . I don't know what they are. And he has funny shoes. they're turned up.

Dr. H.   What is his name?

B. E.   A . . . (Slowly, and then spelling as if reading.) A.B.N. A.B.N. Abn? Abn, something.

Dr. H.   Does he say anything to you?

B. E.   He's telling me to bring the pitcher.

Dr. H.   Are you a servant, or a member of the family?

B. E.   Neither.

Dr. H.   What relationship do you have to him?

B. E.   (With a note of surprise) He owns me.

Dr. H.   You are a slave?

B. E.   Yes, to do things for him. And he always wants to do things to me.

Dr. H.   What does he want to do to you?

B. E.   He wants to hurt me.

Dr. H.   How does he hurt you?

B. E.   He bites me here and here. (Touching her breasts.)

Dr. H.   How old are you?

B. E.   Seventeen.

14

Dr. H. How long have you been with this man?

B. E. Four years.

Dr. H. Did he buy you or did he capture you?

B. E. I don't know.

Dr. H. If you would like to know we can go back and find out.

B. E. (Fearfully) He's cruel.

Dr. H. Do you want to go away from him?

B. E. Yes.

Dr. H. Are you afraid of him?

B. E. Yes, he used to do so many ugly things.

Dr. H. Let's go back to the time when you first met this man. You'll be there at the count of three. 1,2,3.

B. E. He bought me.

Dr. H. Where did he buy you?

B. E. On a big wooden block.

Dr. H. How did you feel about that?

B. E. Afraid.

Dr. H. How did it happen that you were on a big wooden block?

B. E. My father was killed. My mother was killed. Terro ... (As if not sure) Terrorists? Terrorists.

Dr. H. Where were you living?

B. E. In Turkey.

Dr. H. Was it in a city, a village, or a town of any kind?

B. E. It was a village.

Dr. H. Do you know the name of the village?

B. E. No.

Dr. H.   Now return to the time when you were sold.

B. E.   They brought me there from the village on horses.

Dr. H.   Do you know what year it is?

B. E.   Thirteen something.

Dr. H.   As you are being sold on the block, is that the time when the fear first started?

B. E.   No.

Dr. H.   Then go back further to the time when the fear first started. I will count slowly from one to seven. While I an counting you will go back to the beginning of the fear. If we can find the beginning of the fear we can take it all away. 1,2,3,4,5,6,7. Look around you and tell me, your friend and helper, what is happening. I can hear you, but I cannot see what you see. So tell me.

B. E.   I— —don't— —know. There's a little hut with a thatched roof, a chicken and a white goat.

Dr. H.   Do you see any other people around?

B. E.   No (Soft laughter) I'm sitting behind this little . . . this little place. I don't know where. It isn't clear. (Pause) It's hay. Somebody came.

Dr. H.   Who came?

B. E.   A boy. He has a green hat on, and it goes up to a point.

Dr. H.   Can you tell me his name?

B. E.   No.

Dr. H.   Can you tell me your name?

B. E.   I'm not sure.

Dr. H.   Now I'm going to count slowly from one to five to give you time for the picture to clear. You will see clearly all about you. 1,2,3,4,5. The picture is steadily clearing and you know what is happening that caused you to fear. Now tell me.

B. E.   My name is Maureen. I'm fifteen.

Dr. H.   And there was a boy?

B. E.   (Hesitant and blushing) Yes, there's a boy.

Dr. H.   What's happening?

B. E.   I don't want to say.

Dr. H.   Why don't you want to say? Are you ashamed?

B. E.   Because my mother saw us. She told my father and he beat me.

Dr. H.   Did you like this boy?

B. E.   Yes.

Dr. H.   Did you like what you were doing?

B. E.   Yes.

Dr. H.   Did you think it was wrong to be with him?

B. E.   No, I didn't think it was wrong.

Dr. H.   Let's go over this scene again. Go over the entire scene again from the time when the boy first came to you. Tell me the whole story.

B. E.   I was sitting watching the goat and the chicken, and he is coming across the grass. And he has a green hat pointed with a band around it. He has blond hair. He's nineteen and I'm fifteen, and I like him and he likes me. He touches me and it feels good. And he said, "Let's go up in the hay." (Embarassed laughter) And we did, and he's kissing me, and we do something. But it's very nice. And my mother is looking for me and calling me. I didn't answer her and she comes out there and she sees us.

Dr. H.   What did she say?

B. E.   She gets the thatch after me — on my back. She said, "Get inside." And he's frightened and goes away and leaves me. (Disappointment in her

17

voice.)

Dr. H.   How do you feel about that?

B. E.   Then I was afraid.

Dr. H.   Was it because he went away that you are afraid?

B. E.   (Fearfully) No.

Dr. H.   What happened.

B. E.   I was afraid. And my father came home and she told him. (Sobs) He beat me.

Dr. H.   What did he beat you with

B. E.   A leather thing. (Sobbing) He said I wouldn't do that again. Then I had the fear.

Dr. H.   From that time on? (She nods.) Now we are going to go over the entire scene again. Each time you tell it you will find it easier to tell, and as you tell it you will lose you fear. So start again and tell me the whole story.

B. E.   My name is Maureen. I'm fifteen. My mother sent me out to get some eggs. I'm sitting down thinking about him. I have a piece of grass in my mouth, and I'm thinking how beautiful the countryside is. I saw him coming up over the slope. I feel very happy. I like him very much and he likes me very much.

Dr. H.   What does he say to you?

B. E.   Hello, Maureen.

Dr. H.   What do you say to him?

B. E.   Hello.

Dr. H.   Go on, tell the rest of the story.

B. E.   He sat down next to me and took my hand. It felt so sweet and good. And then he kissed me.

Dr. H.   Had he kissed you before?

B. E.   No.

Dr. H.   You liked it?

B. E.   Yes. I had wanted him to. Then we went up into the hay part. And he loved me and I loved him. And mother started calling and I started crying.

Dr. H.   Did you hear her?

B. E.   Yes, but I didn't want to stop. I didn't answer. Then she saw us.

Dr. H.   Then how did you feel?

B. E.   Afraid. She was very angry. She whipped me on the back with the thatch. It's like a broom, but it isn't a broom. She told me to get in there. I guess he was frightened too. I guess that's the reason.

Dr. H.   Did you mother say something to the boy?

B. E.   Something? Something, you scamp. Then he ran. Until then I didn't feel it was wrong.

Dr. H.   Go ahead. What happened?

B. E.   I scrubbed and cleaned the floor. (Long pause.) And I thought. And my daddy came home. (Coughing and sobbing) And he beat me with a leather thing.

Dr. H.   Does he injure you or is it just painful?

B. E.   My back! My back! (As in great pain)

Dr. H.   Do you know what year this is when this is happening?

B. E.   I see some numbers. Eleven . . . . one, one, one, seven.

Dr. H.   Eleven seventeen. Do you know the name of the country in which this is happening?

B. E.   Erin.

Dr. H.   And you are Maureen. What is your last name?

B. E.   O'Flaherty.

Dr. H.   Is the fear all gone?

B. E.   No. But some of it is gone.

With each repetition of the story B. E. would add a few details. And with each telling the emotions diminished so that with the eighth retelling she was speaking in a matter-of-fact tone of voice. I have edited out all but the seventh and eighth relatings of her Maureen O'Flaherty life.

Dr. H.   All right. Now go back to the beginning again. Your mother sent you out for the eggs.

B. E.   I have a long dress on and a little white bonnet. It has a ruffle on it. And I went out to get the eggs. It's a very beautiful day. And I sat down. I was chewing on a piece of grass, and I saw him coming over the slope. His name is Timothy. And he sat down next to me and he held my hand. And he said he liked me. I said I liked him too. Then we went to where all the hay is. We climbed up there. And he kissed me, and he put it between my legs. And it felt very good. Mother is calling me and I couldn't answer. And she saw us and then she hit me and told me to get inside. And then she told him to "Get out of here, you scamp." Then I went in the house. It wasn't a house though. It was a hut. I called it a hut. It has a thatched roof. It has a big wooden table inside. The floor is wooden. There is no stove. There's a big pot and some fire. And I scrub the floor. And my father came and she told him.

Dr. H.   Did you hear her tell him?

B. E.   Yes.

Dr. H.   What were the words she used?

B. E.   Sounds funny. The only words that I hear, "This brat was fooling around with that Dugan boy up in the hay." So he beat me with a piece of leather with a lot of other leather things on it. My back is bleeding. It was painful, but it isn't painful now.

Dr. H.   How about the fear? Is the fear all gone?

B. E.   There's still just a little bit.

Dr. H.   Then tell it one more time and the fear will all be gone. Start at the place where you went out after the eggs.

B. E.   I went out to get the eggs, and it was a beautiful day, And I sat down — —Oh! I forgot to say something!

Dr. H.   Go ahead and say it.

B. E.   I can't.

Dr. H.   Was it something unpleasant?

B. E.   I was touching myself down there.

Dr. H.   Did it feel good?

B. E.   Well, it would have, but then Timmy came over, and so — —(Shyly) I don't think he saw me. And he sat down.

Dr. H.   Did this frighten you?

B. E.   No. I was thinking of him when I was doing that (Laughing)

Dr. H.   Did you like Timmy pretty well?

B. E.   He liked me too. And he held my hand and it was just a beautiful feeling. It was beautiful. Then we went up where all the hay was, and he put it between my legs. And it was just beginning to feel so wonderful, and my mother called. He said, "Don't answer." I didn't answer. Then she saw us. Then she hit me and told me to go inside. And she said, "Get out of here, you scamp." And he left.

Dr. H.   Then how did you feel?

B. E.   I felt very bad.

Dr. H.   Do you feel the fear now?

B. E.   No.

Dr. H.   Is the fear all gone?

B. E.   Yes.

Dr. H.   Then go on with the story.

B. E.   I went in the house, except it wasn't a house. It was a hut. That's what I called it. And I scrubbed the floor. There is a big iron pot hanging. There is a fire under it, and the steam is coming out of it. I'm hungry, but she wouldn't let me have anything to eat.

Dr. H.   How did you feel about that?

B. E.   Well, I was hungry. I didn't mean to be bad.

Dr. H.   Were you being punished for being bad? Is that the reason she wouldn't give you anything to eat?

B. E.   Because of what I was doing, she said.

Dr. H.   And then what happened?

B. E.   And then Father came home and he beat me and he said, "You'll never do that again!" *But I did!* After that I did it with everybody.

Dr. H.   Did you do this with Timmy again?

B. E.   No. With everybody else. I'll show him! But I never enjoyed it any more.

Dr. H.   Tell me about the fear? Is the fear all gone?

B. E.   Yes.

Dr. H.   So you are doing this with everybody else to show your father?

B. E.   Yes. Because he said I would never do it again. He was right. I never had the same feeling. But

I did it!

Dr. H.   Now let's go to the time when you have lived out this life and have left the body of Maureen O'Flaherty. You are able to look back and know and describe what happened. What caused your death?

B. E.   He had red hair and a red beard, and I laughed at him and he choked me.

Dr. H.   How old were you at this time?

B. E.   Thirty-seven.

Dr. H.   Where were you living at the time of your death?

B. E.   Belfast?? (Hesitating) Bel . . .fast.? Belfast.

Dr. H.   Do you know what year it is?

B. E.   It's eleven thirty eight. This man has a long red beard and bushy red hair.

Dr. H.   Are you feeling the fear?

B. E.   No. It's all gone. I don't care. It doesn't make any difference to me. (Almost defiantly) It's no kind of a life anyway.

Dr. H.   You didn't really enjoy it, did you.

B. E.   No. I told you that before. I didn't enjoy it any more.

Dr. H.   You were doing it to spite your father? Is that right?

B. E.   That's right. And when I laughed at him I was really laughing at my father. But he was drunk and he thought I was laughing at him, so he choked me. (With emphasis of finality) AND THAT IS THAT!

Dr. H.   Then what happened after you left this body?
(B. E. sighs deeply several times.)
What's happening now?

23

B. E.   I'm just waiting. (More deep sighs)

Dr. H.   What are you waiting for?

B. E.   Just waiting to come back.

Dr. H.   Do you want to come back?

B. E.   I have to!

Dr. H.   Why do you have to?

B. E.   To make up.

Dr. H.   Who do you have to make it up to?

B. E.   I have to make it up to......to God, to my creator.

Not only did B. E. and others report memory of happenings in previous lives when they wore a different body and different name, but reported also details of between-life happenings and conditions.

To obtain this information, all that was required was a simple question. "What's happening now?" was the one we used most often. Such a question gives the subject complete freedom to respond as they choose. The answers vary widely. Sometimes it is "Nothing." Usually, however, they will give interesting details not only of their state of being, but of specific plans for return to another body. They might detail factors that enter into the choice of their next parents, how they expect to deal with problems previously unsolved and to pass tests previously failed.

Dr. H.   Now go forward in time to the time, the very next time you come back. You will come back and you will describe your coming back as I count to five. 1,2,3,4,5. What is happening now?

B. E.   I'm twelve.

Dr. H.   What is your name?

B. E.   Sahri.

Dr. H.   Where are you living?

B. E.   Turkey.

Dr. H.   Are you living in a city or out in the country?

24

B. E.   In a little village. These men come through — —
          terrorists — — hoards of terrorists — —.

Dr. H.   Then what happened?

B. E.   My mother and father were killed, and I'm very
          frightened.

Dr. H.   Are you feeling this fear now?

B. E.   Yes.

Dr. H.   Tell the story until the fear goes away.

B. E.   I'm twelve. But I'm frightened for so long. It
          won't go away for so long. I'm twelve. My name
          is Sahri. (Fear comes into her voice) These men
          come through. Oh, I don't know.

Dr. H.   Just tell me what happens.

B. E.   They burn the little houses. And they took the
          horses. And they kill my father. And they rape
          my mother, and they kill her with a knife right
          up.

Dr. H.   Did you see this happen?

B. E.   (Weeping) Yes.

Dr. H.   Tell the story again. The fear will go away as
          you tell it. (B. E. began to cry and sob loudly.)
          Now the fear is going away. This happened in
          the past. Tell the story again.

B. E.   (Sobbing begins to diminish.) They burn the
          houses in the village, and they took the horses.
          They killed my father. And they raped my
          mother. And then one of them put a long dagger
          between her legs and pulled it right up cutting
          her open?

Dr. H.   And you felt the fear? (She nods) Do you feel the
          fear now?

B. E.   It's a different fear now because they are
          taking me away. I'm afraid for myself now.

Dr. H.   Go on. Tell me what happened to you.

B. E.   They take me to this square, this town. No, something else. No, for a year....No, they take me back to this town. And my hands are tied behind my back, and I'm tied to a pole — the stake that's stuck in the platform. There are other girls too. And we are all crying. We are all being sold to these people. And this very, very fat man felt me and he bought me. And sometimes he was nice, and sometimes he was not nice. And he travelled about the desert for something. And he had this big, big tent that they would put up in the desert, and put all these rugs down. Beautiful rugs. And he sat on these pillows. He had something around his head. And he wore white — — I don't know what they were. I had never seen them before.

Dr. H.   Was he Turkish?

Although I always tried to avoid leading questions, here is one example of my failure to do this. B. E. promptly reminded me of my error. Her indignation, amounting almost to scorn, is obvious in her voice on the tape recording.

Most writers on the subject of hypnosis claim that the hypnotized subjects obey commands and are easily led by the hypnotist. I have not found this to be the case. My patients have done far more leading of me than I have of them. Now I think in terms of gently leading the subject where the subject wants to go.

It is my aim to base each question after the first on the reply to the previous question. I always also tell the subjects that they are free to refuse to answer if they prefer. By this slower, gentler method, I am sure that we not only make the sessions pleasanter for the subject, but builds a rapport that keeps the subject coming back until the problems are adequately dealt with.

I realize the word *want* can have more than one meaning, or that there can be opposing or contradicting wants in the same person.

This is the way I came to understand our minds after exploring many minds over a span of more than thirty years. I think of the mind as having three facets or areas (each of

26

which is intermingled to a greater or lesser degree with the other two)—the conscious, the subconscious and the superconscious. The conscious area is primarily concerned with sensory experiences, choice making, with receiving impressions through the five senses, caring for the body and possessions, performing work duties, enjoying family and friends or creating art and beauty.

The subconscious level I think of as managing all of the body functions not subject to direct conscious control, such as heart rate, body temperature or glandular function. I also think of the subconscious as the storehouse of memory, as being the part that survives bodily death carrying with it the memory record into the non-physical realm between lives and bringing this memory again into the next body at rebirth.

The third level I think of as the superconscious—that level at which we experience a oneness with all things. When this level is touched, awareness expands without limits. Intuition, inspiration, creativity, have their sources at this level, and when freed up and made available, can be used in any way the conscious mind level chooses.

The surviving subconscious-superconscious has a wider and deeper awareness of the entity's purpose and direction and "wants" to guide the conscious choices so as to facilitate growth, consciousness expansion and total health. When under hypnosis, these "wants" from the non-conscious mind levels are predominant over the contradictory "wants" of the conscious mind.

The hypnotized B. E. exhibited far greater awareness than B. E. in her usual state of consciousness. She would promptly correct me if I did not guide her properly.

With my question, "Was he Turkish?", she became quite indignant and quickly and firmly let me know I was in error.

B. E.   Armenian. *I was Turkish!* I told you *I* was Turkish. I didn't say he was. And I would bring him this urn of wine. Sometimes it would make him nice. When he was nice he would pat my cheek. I would drink some too when he gave it to me. I would dance for him. But sometimes he would get very ugly, and I would be frightened.

Dr. H.   Tell me about the times you were frightened.

27

B. E.   He would rip my clothes off and he would bite me here. (Touching breasts.)

Dr. H.   And you felt the fear?

B. E.   It hurt.

Dr. H.   Is the fear gone now?

B. E.   There's still a little. And he used to hurt me so much down there. I would be sore, and it would hurt so much. He would force and force, and I would bleed. He smelled terrible— —wine, and he was fat and ugly. I was with him for a long time. At first I was almost thirteen. I was with him until I was eighteen.

Dr. H.   Then what happened?

B. E.   Then I died.

Dr. H.   You died at eighteen? What happened to cause your death? (She doubled her right hand as if clutching a dagger and struck herself sharply on the chest.) Did he do it?

B. E.   I did it. I couldn't— —I couldn't— —I just couldn't go on. Because it got so he wouldn't be nice at all. (Repeats stabbing motion.)

Dr. H.   Then what happened? What did they do with the body?

B. E.   (Greatly surprised.) They left it on the desert. I went back there again— —back— —again.

Dr. H.   Back where?

B. E.   Endless, endless, infinite space. Dark, dark, dark. Wanting the light— —wanting the light.

Dr. H.   Do you know why you are in the dark?

B. E.   I *had* to come back again.

Dr. H.   Why did you have to come back?

B. E.   (Speaking very softly, reverently.) To become spiritually perfect.

28

Dr. H.   How did you know that? Did someone tell you?

B. E.   Not in words. I was told, but not in words.

Dr. H.   Were there other beings like yourself waiting to come back?

B. E.   Oh yes! Always, always.

Dr. H.   Did you want to come back?

B. E.   (Most emphatically.) No! I wanted to go there, but I had to come back.

Many attempts have been made to explain away reported past life memories as fantasy, as attempts to please the hypnotist, as recall of something read or seen on TV or film.

It seems to me that the only explanation that fits all the facts of my experience with hundreds of subjects is that we are eternal and live in a series of physical bodies.

I have also been privileged to review a number of my own former lives, was able to see that when in one life there were failures characterized by selfish, selfcentered acts such as refusing to fill a need or ease the pain of suffering ones, such situations are met again — as often as necessary until the lessons are learned and the selfishness has been exchanged for a willingness to serve both other people and whatever Diety we understand. I have had my F grades in the past. I see this life as a chance to raise these failures to passing or better.

My patients too, as they reviewed past experiences, could see where they had made mistakes, how past mistakes were still interfering with their optimum functioning, and how they could make new choices to improve the old error-filled record. Never once did one patient contradict another's basic precepts or even report facts or incidents out of harmony. All demonstrated the applicability of the statement, "Whatsoever a man soweth, that shall he also reap."

Some who came to me straining against life with an attitude that life was unfair, that God played favorites, were led by what was revealed to them from those deeper levels of their minds to accept themselves. and their circumstances. They were also directed by their deeper wisdon to make the choices that would lead to greater awareness, harmony and creativity.

It is a joyful experience and a great privilege to be allowed to witness and participate in this growth of awareness, this developing of harmony, this beauty of creativity.

One theory with which attempts are made to counter evidence of past lives is that this information all comes from the area of fantasy or imagination. It seems to me that this theory is weak. It is unlikely that anyone would fabricate scenes and stories so filled with tragedy and hardship from choice alone. Were the reports filled with love, grandeur, beauty and honor, then the fantasy theory would more likely apply.

Pure fantasy would probably not contain the emotional intensity exhibited as these scenes are reviewed and relived. The emotions displayed actually provide, I believe, the greatest element supporting the validity of the incident as real. I cannot believe anyone could display the intense emotions such as B. E. and others have produced from fantasy alone. For me this is sufficient evidence to constitute proof. For others additional proof may be required.

It is surely more illogical to postulate that all this material has been fabricated than to simply accept it as reported as actual experience from a prior existence.

Whatever its source, this approach helps troubled people — reason enough for its continued use.

Chapter 3

THE FEAR IS BANISHED

*"All fear is painful, and when it conduces not to
safety, is painful without use.—Every considera-
tion, therefore, by which groundless terrors may
be removed, adds something to human happiness."*
Samuel Johnson

Long before I became interested in hypnosis, I had accepted the idea that we live many lives. I don't recall when I
first believed this concept. To me it was the only logical, sen-
sible, reasonable and natural explanation for so many things.
For a long time I was surprised to find people rejecting the
ideas of reincarnation and karma than I was to find those accepting it.

When my patients began telling of happenings from
what they said were former lives under hypnosis, I did not
think it at all strange or remarkable.

Although I find the concepts of reincarnation and karma
completely acceptable, I have little interest in providing
proof for others. I am convinced that others can find
whatever proof they might wish to have by the method of
non-directive hypnotherapy I am detailing here.

As we continued to work with B. E. she again returned to
the life in Scotland as Susan McDonald, and April 17, 1780,
the day of her death in that life. The tape transcript:

B. E.   It's 1780, April 17, in Scotland again.

Dr. H.   Tell me your name.

B. E.   My name is Susan McDonald.

Dr. H.   How old are you?

B. E.   Twenty-five.

Dr. H.   Are you married?

B. E.   Yes.

Dr. H.   Do you have any children?

B. E.   Yes, she's seven years old.

Dr. H.   What is her name?

B. E.   Andrea. Annie. I call her Annie. She has blue eyes and long dark hair.

Dr. H.   Is she pretty?

B. E.   She's so thin. If she wasn't so thin she would be pretty.

Dr. H.   Do you like her?

B. E.   I do, but I'm mean to her. I can't help it.

Dr. H.   Tell me why you can't help it.

B. E.   Because her father doesn't bring us any food. There's never anything to eat.

Dr. H.   What's her father's name?

B. E.   Johnny, Johnathon. I call him Johnny. We're so hungry all the time, and I scream at her because she's hungry and cries and there's nothing I can do. I'm so miserable, so miserable. (Weeping.) So hungry and so cold. There isn't any wood left. Something must be done. Annie and I go down to Gleesbeck's. And he's in there.

Dr. H.   What is he doing?

B. E.   Drinking and laughing and he said to get out. "Get out and leave me alone." I took her home. And on the way....I never could figure this out....there was a large building. It was called the Four Leaf Clover, and there was a clover on the side of it, but it only had three leaves. Every time I passed that building, I can't figure it out why they call it the Four Leaf Clover

32

when they have a picture with only three leaves. It doesn't make sense. It's real stupid. (Laughing) I used to think every time I passed that building that someday, if ever I could get any money, I was going to buy some green paint and come down there some night when it is real dark and put another leaf on that clover. Then it would be the Four Leaf Clover both ways. This used to keep me happy thinking about this and telling Annie about it. Then we went home. This is April 17. This is the day I die again.

Dr. H.   And then what happened?

B. E.   I would tell her how sorry I was because I hit her. It was just to keep her quiet — to keep her from crying. I knew the only reason she was crying was because she was hungry, but I didn't cry and I was hungry too. And then he came home. He had a tankard — a bucket of ale. I took it and threw it clear across the room. And I begged and I pleaded, and he kicked me and then I nagged and nagged. Annie is screaming and crying. And then he pushed me down hard and my head hit the leg of the stove. And that was that. Then he was sorry.

Dr. H.   As you tell the story this time, do you feel the fear?

B. E.   No.

Dr. H.   The fear is all gone?

B. E.   Yes. Let me tell you what happened to him, because it really is quite funny. (Raucous laughter) He kept on drinking and drinking. Some relatives took Annie and raised her and when she was seventeen she married a very nice boy. Aye, he was a nice lad, and she was very happy. But he drank and drank, and so one night he was in Gleesbeck's — —see, I can see — —I'm not there, but I can see all this — —and he became very surly with a man,

33

> and the man hit him and he fell down on this brass railing next to the floor and it killed him. (More strident laughter.) I thought that was so funny because he killed me the same way. That's why it's so funny. Then I was ready to go again. It's getting shorter and shorter.

This report of watching the happenings within the family for more than ten years after her death lends weight to the concept of continuing consciousness after death and continued concern for loved (or hated) ones. This is another area where probing for additional information is an exciting possibility.

There was a short period of silence, B. E. seemed to be in deep thought.

Dr. H.   What's happening now?

B. E.   I went back there again — in the darkness for a long time. I was waiting — waiting.

Dr. H.   What are you waiting for?

B. E.   I have to come back.

Dr. H.   Why do you have to come back?

B. E.   To work this out — that's the only reason I have to come back. Everyone else is waiting too. Some go back when they ask. I keep asking and asking, "Why can't I?" "Time is not yet. Time is not yet."

Dr. H.   You wanted to come back?

B. E.   I *had* to. No, I didn't want to. I had to because I couldn't go where I wanted to go until I was through.

Dr. H.   Where did you want to go?

B. E.   (A note of annoyance in her voice.) With God.

Dr. H.   But you couldn't go there until you were through?

B. D.   No.

34

Dr. H.   You knew this?

B. E.   (Scornfully) Of course! Everyone knew it. That's why everyone is so anxious to get back and get it over with.

Dr. H.   Was there something you still had to do or to learn?

B. E.   Oh, a lot of things.

Dr. H.   What were some of them?

B. E.   To become spiritually perfect, *as I was originally created.*

This concept of having been created spiritually perfect is in complete harmony with the best of theological teachings.

Dr. H.   Did you have any understanding of why you were not spiritually perfect?

B. E.   Yes.

Dr. H.   Can you tell me what that understanding is?

B. E.   Regardless of any of the circumstances, I should have had faith and I didn't. I should have had faith above all, and no fear. The reversal of fear is faith.

Dr. H.   Are you going to make it this time?

B. E.   I'm going to try. All I can do is try.

Dr. H.   Tell me about coming back.

B. E.   I'm in B......, North Dakota, at my mother's mother's farm house. I'm being born. He's pulling me out of my mother. (She winces as in pain and places her hands to the sides of her head.)

Dr. H.   Is there something around your head?

B. E.   (With a sigh of relief.) Metal

Dr. H.   Are you aware of what is happening in the room?

B. E.   Oh yes.

Dr. H.   Tell me about it.

B. E.   My mother is in anguish.

Dr. H.   Has this been a long difficult birth?

B. E.   Yes, fourteen hours. He has a long gray beard. I said this before.

Dr. H.   Yes you did. Tell me again.

B. E.   And gray hair and glasses. And my mother is exhausted. (Sudden merry laughter.)

Dr. H.   What's so funny?

B. E.   I can remember everything, you see, from before, but they don't know I can remember. (More exhuberant laughter.) And I can't tell them that I can remember.

Dr. H.   Big joke, isn't it?

B. E.   I never did like warm cows milk. But I'm hungry — — so what are you going to do? But then, I should complain—I was so hungry before.

Dr. H   They fed you warm cows milk?

B. E.   My grandmother brought it to me in a bottle. My mother's mother.

Dr. H.   How did you let them know when you were hungry?

B. E.   WAAAAAAAA! WAAAAAAAAAAA! How else? (More laughter.) I could relay thoughts, but they couldn't catch them. That was the trouble. There wasn't anything wrong with me. I could fling them out all right. They just couldn't—Non compus mentis!

Dr. H.   That is a big joke.

B. E.   It's all right being a baby, if you just didn't think so much. But then there isn't much else you can do. You can't walk. You can't talk. You can just think.

Another area for research — Do babies think? Traditionally we view the minds of newborns as a blank page — hardly containing much material with which to think. Additionally it would be valuable to determine the extent to which babies and young children are aware of family circumstances and attitudes. B. E. reported being aware both before and immediately after birth of conditions of her environment.

Dr. H.   What are you thinking about?

B. E.   Growing up, getting busy and getting it over with.

Dr. H.   You say you can remember everything from before. Can you remember what is happening in your home before you were born. Can you remember how your father and mother felt about you coming?

B. E.   He said he didn't want any God-damned brat. That's the reason she didn't want me, I guess.

Dr. H.   But they were married?

B. E.   Yes, she was very young. I think she was seventeen when they got married, nineteen when I was born. Jesus, after two years they should have known what to do if they didn't want any, I guess.

Dr. H.   Can you describe how you felt when you found out they didn't want you?

B. E.   Oh, that didn't make a damn bit of difference to me. I still had to come back to those particular people.

My patients often report that people that they are involved with in the present life have been known to them in other lives. The relationships can change widely from lifetime to lifetime. The answers they give me supports the concept that unfinished business in one life must be finished in a later life with the same people.

Dr. H.   Where had these people entered into your expe-

37

riences previously?

B. E.   Oh! I didn't know 'til just now. My mother was Annie.

Dr. H.   And your father?

B. E.   Johnathon!

Dr. H.   So you had to come back to Johnny and Annie again.

B. E.   Yes.

Dr. H.   Had there been other times when these same two people had been with you before?

B. E.   (After a long pause) Timothy. (In great surprise.)

Dr. H.   Who was Timothy?

B. E.   Timothy Dugan, and Johnathon and my father.

Dr. H.   Now Annie and your mother — were there any other times when this soul was with you?

The next development came to me as a surprise. B. E. had said that the fear was all gone and had been calm and relaxed for some time. But suddenly in response to this question she began to roll from side to side and wail loudly as if in great torment.

B. E.   NO, NO, NO, NO! oh no!

Dr. H.   What is it?

B. E.   (The wailing continuing and gaining force.) NO NO NO!

Dr. H.   You can relax, because it is all past (another mistake.) Now you know why these things have come into your experience.

B. E.   My daughter! And my mother! Oh! Oh no! No. NO!

Dr. H.   Do you mean that your daughter, Susan, and Annie and your mother are all the same soul?

B. E.   Yes. What did you say? I was thinking.

Dr. H.   Is this correct that Susan and Annie were the same . . .?

B. E.   Susan was my mother. My mother was Annie.

Dr. H.   And then she was your mother?

B. E.   And now she's Susan.

Dr. H.   Was she the same mother that you had when you were Maureen?

B. E.   (After long pause.) Annie—and I beat that little thing!

Dr. H.   You say that she beat you when you were Maureen, and then you beat her when she was Annie. Will it be her turn next time?

B. E.   Let me see now. No!! You know why?

Dr. H.   Why?

B. E.   Because Susan is my daughter now, and I don't beat Susan. I love her and take good care of her.

Dr. H.   Now let us go back to the time when you were a little girl. You are still remembering. You are not yet three years old. Somewhere during this time you get a little brother. A little brother comes to live with you . . Tell me about the time when you get a little brother.

B. E.   (Sudden childish snort and giggle.) Uh, uh. I didn't like him. I was jealous. (More childish laughter.)

Dr. H.   How old are you when you get a little brother?

B. E.   Not quite two.

Dr. H.   What is his name?

B. E.   Robert.

Dr. H.   What did you call him?

B. E.   (Childishly) But-tee.

Dr. H.   Now you can remember all the things from the

past. So you know whether you have known Robert before. You remember, and that will help you understand why you don't like him. In times past did Robert have another name?

B. E.   (Very slowly and solemnly.) Abn.

Dr. H.   So you were Robert's slave once, and you didn't like him then. Now he has come back to be with you, and you know what this means to you. What is it that you must do about this relationship with Robert?

B. E.   Well, the first thought is that I would have would be to get back at him — to hurt him in some way as he hurt me. But I know that that is not it. Because then I would have to keep on and on and on. So, I think the thing to do would be to act like a good sister, be kind and loving and to let him know that I love him as a brother, and expect the same from him. And if I expect it and if I put a little bit of it out, I'm certain that it will come back tenfold.

Dr. H.   Did you put a little bit of it out, as you say?

B. E.   I don't think that I felt any .... ever felt any ... for evidently I knew up until I was three. So I suppose that before I was three I must have put an awful lot of hostility somewhere in my mind. So when the time came and I couldn't remember, I'd have something to show.

Dr. H.   Now that you know the whole story, do you realize that you will have to learn to love Robert too?

B. E.   Yes, of course. (Long pause while a thoughtful expression played across her face.) Before I was two I tried to bite his penis off. (Laughter.) He was about a month old.

Dr. H.   Do you know why you did this?

B. E.   Why sure.

40

Dr. H.   Why did you do it?

B. E.   Because before he was always making me hurt down there. I was going to fix it so that he couldn't make someone else hurt. (More laughter.)

Dr. H.   But you didn't succeed?

B. E.   Mom caught me.

Dr. H.   What did she do?

B. E.   She didn't spank me.

Dr. H.   Did she know you were trying to bite it off?

B. E.   I don't know whether she did or not.

Dr. H.   But you meant it?

B. E.   I meant it! But then he's okay, I guess.

Dr. H.   Now we are going forward in time a little ways to the time you were about six years old — to the last scenes pertaining to your father. You will tell me about that event, and as you tell it the last fragments of fear that you have had for so long are going to drop away.

  I will count to six and you will be six years old. 1,2,3,4,5,6. Now tell the story one more time about the last part of your father's life.

B. E.   He drank an awful lot all of the time. We were hungry again. Mother wasn't working. They were very young. We lived in a brown house, and he was mean, but I loved him. He was my Daddy. But he would go down in the basement and shut off the gas. They would argue and fight all the time — all the time. So Mama finally got disgusted, I guess. Buddy and I were sick. We had double pneumonia or something like that. Mustard plasters all over the place. So she took us across — — about a block to the Lacey's, because he had been drinking and she was afraid of him. I remember her saying that to Mrs. Lacey. Mrs. Lacey said, "Now don't you

41

worry. You just stay right here and I'll take care of everything." They had three or four children so there wasn't an extra bedroom. Buddy and I were on this brown leather davenport which opened into a bed and he came in there, drunk. He told Mama to come home and bring us home. And she said "No", that she would not. She would never come back again. And then he went out. It was snowing. It was very cold. and then he came back again, and he chased her around, pushed her outside, started to beat her and chased her around this lot. He kicked her between the legs from the back. Buddy and I were looking out of the window. We were screaming and crying for him not to hurt our Mommy. I can remember seeing the blood— the red blood—on the snow. even though it was at night it was very bright out and the snow was sort of blue. And we were screaming and crying and I was afraid. And then he walked off across the lot, and she crawled on her hands and knees into the house. Mrs. Lacey called the police. And he came back in just a few minutes and he said that he was going to ask her for the last time, and if she would not come home—he took a bottle of Lysol out of his coat, a gray coat, pocket—and he said, "If you don't come home and bring the kids I am going to drink this." She said, "I am not coming back." And he took the stopper off, and he drank it. He got very white and frothy around his mouth. And we were watching and we were crying, and we were screaming and we were afraid. And he fell down on the floor. And Mama and Mrs. Lacey tried to put some raw eggs down his throat. Then the police came in—it seems that the police came first and then an ambulance came. I think it was the ambulance driver who looked at him and said, "It's too late. He's dead." And I felt very sad because my Daddy was gone.

Dr. H.   As you tell the story now, do you feel the fear?

B. E.   No, It's all gone. Then they took him away. And that is the end of the story.

Dr. H.   Since the fear is all gone, you don't need to tell the story again. I am going to bring you forward in time to the present, to 1956, back to my office, back to an active phase and you will soon completely awaken. We will discuss the whole experience. You will remember everything. You will know how each event fits into each other event. You are coming forward slowly. You feel relaxed and comfortable. You have just had an experience in which you have recalled many things and have relived old fears until the fears were gone. The fear need never return. You are awake now. How do you feel?

B. E.   Things are shaping up!

Dr. H.   Do you feel pretty good right now?

B. E.   I feel—well, I have to pee. (Laughter.)

When B.E. awakened and sat up her appearance was markedly changed from the fear-ridden woman who first came to me. She was now calm and composed, with a quick smile and sparkling eyes. Her expression was one of enthusiastic optimism.

There were still other problems which we dealt with later. But in these two short sessions we had probed to find the cause of her panic, had found it and had relieved the emotional pressure to the extent that she no longer needed the daily drinking.

Certainly B. E.'s present life contained enough violence to fill her with fear. An unwanted child, she had witnessed the constant discord, nagging and fighting of her parents. Violence and hate had surrounded her. The peak of violence was the day of her father's suicide, a day filled with fighting, threats, beating, tearful pleadings and finally the drinking of the poison in front of her. She had watched his death agonies. Such a series of events would of course have struck fear in her heart.

It might be argued that this experience alone was the basis of B.E.'s fear, and I am sure many would take this position. And those same people would contend that the other lives she reported — lives of violence — were only fantasies or remembered present life experiences. However, it is illogical to make this claim. There was no obvious reason for the creating of fantasies. She certainly was under no compulsion from us to create "a tall story." There was not even a suggestion. She made it plain that she was *not* trying to please the hypnotist.

Instead of a need to disguise, or complicate, or confuse some so-called "real " situation in this life by devising stories about another life, the real need was for simplification and exploration of present life situations. If the situations of this life were the basis of her fears, if the violence she experienced in this life were all of the story, she would have had no motivation to bring up other lives.

According to the material which B. E. presented she had been involved in lives of violence with the same souls for more than 800 years. During this time she had four lives — as B. E., as Susan McDonald, as Sahri and as Maureen O'Flaherty. The soul who had been her mother in 1117 had become her daughter in 1780 and was both her mother and her daughter in her present life.

The soul who had been Timothy, a boy who first loved her, but then ran away to leave her to face punishment alone, which in turn drove her into an immoral life which ended by her being choked to death by a red-bearded drunk, became her husband, Johnny in 1780. As the husband he left her and their daughter in hunger and in cold, and finally killed her in a drunken rage. In this life as B. E. she was again associated with the same soul as her father. Again the pattern repeated — rejection, beating, drunkenness and suicide as she watched with childish eyes.

The soul who had been the fat, ugly merchant, Abn, who had bought her as his slave after she had witnessed the rape and pillage of her home village, returned again as her baby brother.

All these lives were crowded with hate, lust, violence, crime and death. It would seem that if B. E. were making up tales about her former existences she would have at least put in something of love, of beauty, of satisfaction.

Wherever the material came from, it served a most useful purpose. Once B. E. understood the basis for her fear and panic, and had been able to release the long-buried emotions attached to the original incidents, the fear was gone. The panic had vanished. There was no longer a need for her to drink daily to be able to cope with the fear. She was now able to work full days at her job, without being required to hurry to a bar to avoid running and screaming down the street. Certainly not all of B.E.'s problems were solved as if by magic. But those problems which compelled her to seek help were now reduced to a level of toleration. I knew that as she continued to integrate her new-found knowledge, they would fade into the untroublesome memories of her past where they, like the ripples of the stone dropped into the ocean, become lost in the larger and more recent ripples of living. Yet, also like the ripples which are never really lost, but continue to exert their force forever, remain forever a part of the ceaseless movements of the sea of her life.

They, like all of the experiences of all of our life, or all of our lives, are the substances with which we each build our own eternity.

Chapter 4

WEIGHING THE EVIDENCE

"Hear one side, and you will be in the dark; hear both sides and all will be clear."   Thomas C. Haliburton

After just these two therapy sessions, B.E. was completely relieved of the urge to run and scream. Her recurrent panic was totally alleviated. She could now put in full days at work. She no longer had to leave her desk at midafternoon to go get a few drinks. The drinking stopped because the need to drink was gone.

All previous treatment she had received had failed to give any relief. I doubt if any treatment other than the approach used in my office could have helped.

There were other problems on which we worked in subsequent sessions. None were of the magnitude of the panic. When she moved from my part of the country several months later she was a woman at peace with herself. I am sure that any other method of therapy would have been far less effective for her. Other methods surely would not have helped so quickly.

Rapid response on the part of patients is very important to me. It seems cruel to use slower methods when prompt relief of suffering is easily obtainable using non-directive hypnotherapy.

What I am presenting here does not constitute proof. My critics demand proof. I admit that I cannot furnish it to them. However, I believe any physician, psychologist, counsellor or other therapist can find their own proof if they ask the right questions.

I have found the ideas of Reincarnation and Karma acceptable for most of my life. I became more interested when I read *There is a River*, by Thomas Sugrue, a biography of

Edgar Cayce. Further interest was aroused by *Many Mansions*, by Gina Cerminara, when the book first appeared in 1950. This book too dealt with the psychic work of Edgar Cayce, an uneducated young man who, when in hypnosis, manifested remarkable and unusual abilities. He spent nearly forty-five years going into deep hypnotic states and giving "readings" for those who sought his help. Most of the "readings" had to do with diagnosing and recommending treatment for people who were ill. About midpoint of these forty-five years, he began to include the concept of Reincarnation and Karma in his work—emphasizing that "Whatsoever a man soweth, that shall he also reap."

My interest grew. I wanted to be more sure. I wanted to prove it to myself. Never is it enough for me to accept an idea just because I read it or hear it spoken.

The obvious proof would be to use hypnosis and ask questions, I reasoned. This I did—recalling first several of my own former lives, each of which added greatly to my self-understanding in this life. I also began working with hypnosis, first with family and friends, and then cautiously with patients.

Since 1950, when I began to use hypnosis, I have collected a vast amount of information from the many persons with whom I have worked. This information has proved to be always harmonious with itself and with the material produced by the sleeping Edgar Cayce. Never once did one patient contradict another. Neither did they produce anything contradictory to the Edgar Cayce material. It seems reasonable to me to conclude that unless these ideas are valid, some patient at some time would have given contradictory statements or facts during these thirty-plus years.

I have evidence that satisfies my requirement of proof. Anyone else can find the same.

I am here describing my methods and relating my findings. This is an investigation into the human mind that is repeatable by any interested investigator. Granted, research using human subjects is not repeatable in the same way as research using small animals. Most psychological research using rats or other small animals may be repeatable and may give some information about human behavior. It is hard for me to accept the premise that information obtained from rat research gives any real information about the human mind.

To really understand the *human* mind and *human* behavior, research findings need to be checked on human subjects, no matter how difficult it may be to maintain all of the "controls" so sacred to scientific researchers.

Hypnosis is a tool for human research. Techniques for inducing hypnosis are easily learned. Willing research subjects are readily available. My work can be repeated by anyone who cares to repeat it.

Proof is whatever we require it to be. There will be those who will reject my findings — even their own findings if such evidence falls counter to preconceived ideas of the nature of life and of the universe.

My hope is that future research be aimed at discovering what *is* — not just at providing support for previously cherished beliefs.

Not only have we found that the material many of our subjects produced contained evidence for reincarnation, but have also found this idea to be extremely helpful in enabling the subject to cope with life problems. Our subjects were guided to seek within to find the causes of their problems. They were instructed to go to any time or place that would give answers to their questions. They would find their own direction. They would tell themselves causes of problems. They would demand of themselves the full acceptance of responsibility for their own life. They would stop blaming others. This has proved to be psychologically healing, growth promoting, awareness expanding.

Our subjects, after experiencing this approach to therapy, report feeling free of compulsion, able to make choices without former conflicts born of fear, hate, guilt, sorrow or other strong feelings. Again and again they quote or paraphrase the statement, "You will know the truth and the truth shall make you free."

Traditional hypnotherapy emphasizing the use of suggestion alone to produce behavioral changes falls far short of this result. Suggestion alone can and does have a beneficial potential. Hypnosis alone without even suggestions is helpful in that it enables the subject to relax and be less filled with stress.

However, suggestion as usually applied in directive

hypnotherapy, leaves untapped a vast resource within the subject. Within each person is an unlimited supply of self-knowledge, wisdom, strength, creativity and capacity for abundant living.

When a non-directive approach is used, this source is contacted, and from it comes all requested information. Here is a source easily tapped that can tell us whatever is causing a difficulty and also what needs to be done to resolve the problem. Unfortunately this source is too infrequently tapped.

Many of my subjects when asked to find the cause of their difficulty or illness reported finding the cause in a previous lifetime in another body. Some located the cause in an early period of their present life.

The very large body of such evidence demands examination if not acceptance.

Subject after subject would follow closely a common pattern. I would instruct them to go back and find any happening or experience that caused or helped to cause their problem. I did not specifically request that they go back to another life.

Whether in this life or a former life, the process appears to be the same. A scene (usually accompanied by a strong emotion) will begin to unfold. Sometimes the emotion would precede the scene. As they would begin to describe whatever was happening, the emotions displayed were unmistakeably real. This was no mere fantasy or simple memory recall. The subjects were obviously living what they were describing.

As the experiences are repeated again and again, the emotion diminishes in intensity and the patient becomes free of the problem.

I do not propose this as proof—only as evidence that there is a method that works—often very rapidly—to relieve a great variety of patients of their need for a physician.

This is the way it works for me. I have taught others my method and it has worked the same way for them. I do not claim to understand all of the reasons this method produces the results I relate here.

Further research may add to this understanding which already surpasses our understanding of how many medicines work.

Hippocrates once said, "...it is impossible to make all the sick well."

I am wondering how he would respond to the statements made here and to the cases which I shall describe. As a brilliant physician, I can imagine that he would thoroughly examine my data, then repeat the techniques described with his own patients.

I would expect him to candidly and courageously relate his findings and challenge all detractors to disprove his conclusions.

Perhaps this ancient statement remains true. I contend that we do not know the extent of its truth until *all* available therapies have been used.

My own record with reportedly "incurable" cases strongly suggests that many if not all sick can be made well. Hypnosis, properly used, is a means by which the number being made well can be greatly enlarged.

Early in my practice, I confronted the question of the "incurable" and was dissatisfied with what I realized. I was not helping people in the way I had hoped and planned to do during medical school years. When I prescribed a tranquilizer, I felt I was failing — not really helping.

Not until I began using hypnosis regularly was I satisfied that my patients were really being helped. Then I could see the improvement and could know that these changes were long-lasting — even permanent. The changes were no longer limited to the effects of a pill.

The patients began getting well — or at least needing to visit me less often. The appointment book became less crowded. I was able to have the time to talk with each patient.

Those doctors who claim that they don't have time to talk to patients haven't really tried using hypnosis. My experiences with hypnosis demonstrates unmistakeably that here is a way of speeding up treatment rather than lengthening it. The following cases will illustrate this.

Mrs. A. W. was referred to me by her physician who had already tried everything available to him without results. She was pregnant with her second child. The pregnancy was going well except that she had been vomiting daily for four and one-half months. This vomiting had persisted even though every known medical treatment except hypnosis had been used.

I interviewed her, taking a history and testing her for hypnotizeability on the first visit. I had long suspected that persistent vomiting of pregnancy had an emotional cause. I questioned her at length. She denied that there was tension in her life. She claimed to be completely happy with her marriage. Her children were spaced exactly as she had wished. There were no worries about money, her home or her relatives. "If I would just stop vomiting, my life would be perfect." she insisted.

During the hypnotizeability test she responded very quickly and reached a deep state of hypnosis with spontaneous amnesia.

Her appointment a few days later went as follows: I asked her to lie down on the therapy couch, gave her the prearranged signal for her to go into deep hypnosis. Within ten seconds she was in a deep state. I turned on the tape recorder, turned to her and said, "Tell me why you are vomiting."

A frown crossed her face, a note of irritation entered her voice. She said, "To get even with my husband."

When I asked why she wanted to get even with her husband, she drew her shoulders up in a haughty gesture, gave her head a toss and responded, "Well! We're Mormons. We're taught that if our children are to be our children in the next life our marriage must be blessed in the Temple. He doesn't think that is important and he won't go through with it. And the only way I can upset him as much as *that* upsets me is to vomit."

I wakened her from the hypnosis, called her husband into the room, and played the tape recording to them. As soon as A.W. heard her voice she exclaimed—pointing to the recorder—"That's my voice!" As she listened to the words she had just spoken her eyes widened in amazement. Her mouth gaped. Tears began to pour down her cheeks as she pleaded with me and her husband with the words. "I didn't *know* I felt that way! *Please believe me.* I didn't know I felt that way."

We both assured her of this belief and she regained her composure. She was now equipped with new information to deal with the vomiting. She was free to choose. She could now continue it to upset her husband as before or she could stop the vomiting.

She reported that she stopped vomiting. I never learned whether her marriage was blessed in the Mormon Temple or whether she found a new way to upset her husband. She came to me for help with the vomiting—a condition that had persisted for four and one-half months and had resisted all medical treatment.

The therapy session in my office took less than five minutes. The vomiting stopped and did not recur. Her referring physician could have done the same thing and thereby saved himself and his patient a great deal of both time and expense. He could have spared his patient months of daily vomiting.

The fact that it is this easy thoroughly refutes the argument that doctors don't have time to use hypnosis.

An even better example of the time economy of using hypnotherapy is the case of Mrs. C.R., a woman aged 52 who had suffered a persistent affliction for 45 years.

She had frequent episodes—always one or more annually—during the entire 45 years of heavy gasping for breath. This frantic gasping would persist day and night, and would result in total exhaustion. In order to control these episodes she would have to be heavily sedated, sometimes for several days and often in a hospital setting. Some episodes had even required general anesthesia. Sedatives or anesthesia would help to stop one episode, but did not effect the frequency or the severity of subsequent attacks. Her frustrated physician sent her to me with the words, "If you can do anything for this woman I will be most grateful." (None of us physicians enjoy being confronted again and again with our failures.)

During the initial interview she related that at the time her problem developed at age 7 years, she also began refusing to go to school. When she was spanked so much that she chose school as the lesser evil, she would follow a very long route to the school rather than the shortest path which led down through a gulley or wash. She could not recall any event either related to the school or the gulley that would account for her 45 years of affliction. She responded well to hypnotizeability tests and returned the next day for her first, and only, therapy session. She was helped into a medium level of hypnosis. I then asked her to move back in time to age seven to any happening that caused the gasping.

She began at once to describe a morning when she, aged seven, and her best friend, Nancy, were on the way to school. They had taken the shortcut through the gully. Suddenly, from behind a large bush leaped a fifteen your old feeble minded fourth grader named John. John grabbed both girls and almost succeeded in raping C.R. She escaped from John and ran until she dropped in exhaustion gasping for breath. She had blocked out all conscious memory of this rape attempt. The emotion had remained. This persistent emotion had sparked her gasping attacks over the many years.

During the first reliving of the near-rape — and she was telling of the event in the present tense — she screamed, she cried, she struggled. I asked her to go through the experience again from the beginning. This time the emotional outbursts were less extreme.

In this case it was necessary to have C.R. repeat the reliving of the causative event seven times — for a total of eight. Each time I asked her to add any details that she had left out with the previous telling. Each repeat expended more of the emotion. With the eighth reexperiencing, she was describing the incident in a calm matter-of-fact manner. The emotion had all been drained away. After each repeat I had asked her if the fear was gone. Only after the eighth time through it did she respond with a "yes". I awakened her after telling her that she would remember all that she had related.

She awakened with a broad smile saying, "I really feel different. I feel so much better. The pressure is gone. And to think that I have carried that for 45 years. And at such a cost."

I could not estimate the countless hours of doctor's time, the thousands and thousands of dollars of medical and hospital costs that this case had required. I had spent about two hours with her. The first hour for history and hypnosis testing and training. The second — the only therapy session — the only one that was needed. The severe gasping episodes left her and did not return.

This is no claim to magic. I am only trying to illustrate that people with long-lasting and resistent problems can often be helped in a very short time using non-directive hypnotherapy. Much time and money can thereby be saved. A vast amount of suffering can be eliminated. It seems to me that this is the true purpose and calling of the physician. For me anything less is not enough.

I make no claim that all patients respond this quickly. One of my most interesting cases was one with which I worked over a period of six years. This is the Anne Armstrong case, details of which are in the next chapter. I learned a lot from Anne, and I found extreme satisfaction in working with her problems.

Other patients required different lengths of time. For some, two or three sessions would be enough. For others once or twice a week for several months would be required. Anne Armstrong was the only one with whom I worked, albeit intermittently, for a long period of time. With her we probed much deeper into her memory for more than just the cause of the migraine headaches that had brought her to me at first. We also learned a great deal about the mind in this exploration. Her willingness and curiosity were a great asset to the explorations. I have been most grateful that I was a party to the search we conducted within her.

As I review in my mind the series of faces of patients who came to me — drawn, tense, frightened, worried, in pain, ill — a wide scope and variety of people are represented — people in distress. They had come seeking release. I am sure none of them cared very much how the release came so long as it came. After hypnotherapy, most of them were smiling, relaxed, happy, grateful and well. This is not true of everyone. Some remained deeply troubled. Either I had not done the thing which was right for them, or there was an element of faith that did not suffice.

Another possible explanation for the failure to respond could be that the patient resisted the self-knowledge that was necessary for the relief of their problems. This too falls within the scope of the non-provable. I prefer to think that we simply did not probe deeply enough.

One of my near failures was a young woman, N.W. with severe asthma. Her condition had for years varied from severe to moderate and back to severe. She could not work and frequently required hospitalization during the severe episodes.

I worked with her for several months. The asthma symptoms moderated slightly, but were still very much with her. Whenever I would ask her to go back in time to find the cause of her illness, she would begin to describe a scene and then would remark, "It's all gone black." or "There's nothing more." For N.W. and a few other I found it necessary to use a more potent therapy modality.

This method is the use of inhalation of a mixture of 30% Carbon Dioxide and 70% Oxygen — a technique developed by Dr. L. J. Meduna, of Chicago. This gas mixture is called carbogen and is used for a number of conditions. It produces a very rapid and profound change in consciousness. A one minute treatment is often long enough.

N.W. accepted my suggestion to try carbogen. The inhalation mask was placed over nose and mouth and the carbogen was turned on. One minute — thirty five breaths — later she sat up on the couch, clutched at my shoulders, and clinging frantically began to scream. Never before nor since have I heard such screaming.

I will admit that at first I was at a loss as to what I should say or do. I am glad for what I did. I simply held her in my arms and waited. The screaming continued, gradually diminishing in intensity for about forty-five minutes. Then followed several minutes of heavy sobbing.

Finally she was able to speak and said, "I want to tell you what happened." I responded, "I want you to tell me what happened."

"I was in a theater. There was a fire and a panic. I was trampled to death. I wanted to scream then, but I couldn't because there were all these feet on me!"

She rested a few minutes and as she was leaving remarked that the asthma seemed to be gone. Indeed it was gone. She needed no further therapy.

I remained in touch with this patient for ten years after this treatment. She remained well. From the day of the screaming the asthma was gone and it did not return. She was able to return to college, to resume her art studies including sculpture. She wrote me that she had entered her art in eleven exhibitions and had won a prize in every one. It is indeed gratifying to see an incapacitated patient be able to return to normal activity in so short a time.

I made no attempt to identify the date or place of the reported theater fire, panic, nor to learn her name in that life. For me it is enough that the patient's health improves. Whether what is reported is fantasy or fact is far less important to me than the long range effect. I have come to accept what my patients report as valid. However, if one chooses to build and report a fantasy, I also accept that as a valuable part of therapy. A few of my patients have begun with fantasy material and then would abruptly change in tone and begin to recall and relive actual previous happenings.

My tape files contain enough evidence to fill many volumes. To the doubter, this will still not suffice.

This is not *proof.* It is evidence of great weight and persuasion to all but the closed-minded. Should I detail every case, it would still not convince the opponents of such ideas.

I feel that for each of us the most convincing evidence is that which is individually produced.

I hope that this and other chapters will present a challenge to other psychotherapists to use non-directive hypnotherapy and produce their own evidence.

Chapter 5

ANNE ARMSTRONG

Forever from the hand that takes
One blessing from us others fall
And soon or late, our Father
Makes his perfect recompense for all

Whittier

From the beginning, my association with Anne Armstrong was unusual. I met her quite by chance. I was giving a lecture and hypnosis demonstration at the Fair Oaks Community Center near Sacramento, California in the fall of 1959. I called for volunteers from the audience. Anne came forward, a small dark woman in her late thirties. We had never met before, though she said she had heard of me through a neighbor.

When asked, she explained that she had suffered severe migraine headaches for almost her entire life. These headaches had defied all medical treatment and were now appearing almost every day.

She was quick to respond, and was soon in a deeply relaxed state. I asked her to go back to the time her headaches started, expecting her to report some happening from her childhood as another migraine patient had recently done.

Instead, she began to cry out, to moan, to writhe about as if in agony. Her appearance and her behavior were that of a person in great torment or anguish. I reasoned that she was in a state of hysteria, reassured her that she was all right, suggested that she cry as much as she needed to. After a few minutes the moaning and writhing stopped, she became quiet and I awakened her. I asked her to see me the next day in my office.

57

When she came to my office, she was somewhat agitated. She was reluctant to repeat the experience of the evening before, but she was also curious about why she had behaved so strangely — so differently from the calm exterior that she usually wore.

We were soon able to begin unravelling the mystery. What had happened on that platform the evening before was a very sudden and profound change. She had found herself to be in a huge male body that was being stretched and torn on a torture rack.

Further probing filled in the blanks. She relived and described incidents from the life of a superb Roman athlete, Antonius, who was protege and bodyguard of Julius Caesar. He was totally loyal to Caesar and stood in the way of those who plotted Caesar's death. The plotters framed Antonius, arrested him, tortured him on the rack and finally dragged him behind a chariot by the neck until dead.

We spent many hours going over the life of Antonius covering his childhood and youth. Anne in hypnosis was able to relate even minute details of Roman life and of Antonius' family, friends and daily activities. Were I to include all of the transcripts, I would have to write several volumes.

The headaches began to diminish both in severity and frequency as our probing continued. However, they failed to disappear completely.

I remarked one day, "I wonder what Antonius did to deserve this." Anne responded, "I don't think I want to know."

We continued to develop more details of the life of Antonius. Further information included the death of his father in a chariot accident when Antonius was only eight. As the oldest of three children, Antonius took over the responsibility of supporting his mother and brothers by working in the arena. At first his duties were menial such as cleaning the animal stalls and being servant to the gladiators. He spent nearly ten years around the arena with ever greater responsibilities.

By age eighteen he was six foot five inches tall and weighed about 265 pounds. His duties included caring for the horses and chariots and putting away the athletic equipment after the gladiatorial games. He did more that just care for them. He began to practice with the javelin and discus — then on to trying the chariots after everyone had left.

One day as dusk fell, Antonius was joyously driving the best chariot team through complicated trick turns totally oblivious to everything except the thrill of pounding hooves and wind in his face — of perfection in his performance.

Unnoticed, Caesar, himself, had entered the arena and had observed the superb skill of the young man handling the powerful team. He was so greatly impressed with the young man that he invited him to the palace for an interview. Antonius was so embarrassed he stammered and tried to refuse saying that he had no clothes that were suitable for a visit to the palace. Caesar answered that he was to go to a certain gate where proper clothing would be provided.

When Antonius went to the palace the following day he was not only given beautiful soft white garments, but was bathed repeatedly until he was deemed fit to be in Caesar's presence. During the interview, Antonius was offered the chance to represent Caesar as his personal gladiator in the arena games.

Almost overwhelmed by the offer, Antonius accepted joyously. He had never dreamed of being in such a grand place or in the presence of such a great person. All was not smooth, however. One member of the court, whom Antonius called "Fancy Pants" because of his penchant for elaborate flashy clothes, was jealous of Antonius. "Fancy Pants" even went to his house to try to dissuade Antonius from accepting the offer. Antonius was not to be dissuaded. The jealousy within "Fancy Pants" grew and grew. It was "Fancy Pants" who gave the orders to the brutes in the torture chamber to tighten the wheel tighter and tighter.

We also developed details of many other lives besides Antonius. Each contributed to her understanding of herself, but the headaches persisted. Anne finally decided that she wanted to trace the headaches to their source.

It was with great reluctance that Anne agreed to look all the way to the source not only of the headaches, but also for the reason for the suffering of Antonius.

I asked her to go back as far as necessary to find the answers we were seeking. The opening scene was one in which she (this time in a female body) was on a high platform looking out over a crowd of hundreds of people. She recognized herself as a very powerful ruler dominating her subjects by fear and the use of her extraordinary supernatural abilities. She had begun by using her powers for the benefit of her people, but then got off on the wrong track and began to use them only for her own gain and amusement. She became more and more obcessed with the control she wielded over her people.

She described herself as being tall, slender and very beautiful. She wore elegant, but often transparent gowns. Her breasts were usually bare and painted to match her gown. She told of having a group of male slaves who were servants and playthings for her. However, one slave was uncooperative. He would defy her requests and even called her an evil woman.

This so infuriated her that she made special plans for him. She ordered a special golden hammer and spike made. Then she arranged an elaborate banquet. To entertain her banquet guests she had the defiant slave carried in an a plank and drove the golden spike through his head with the golden hammer.

When this session was finished, Anne exclaimed, "I know that is it. Every time I have a headache it feels like someone is driving a spike through my head."

We continued working on that life as the black priestess-ruler for several weeks. The headaches became far less frequent and severe. When I asked her where that slave of the golden spike had entered into her other experiences, she recognized him first as "Fancy Pants," who was the undoing of Antonius, and then as Jim, her husband in her present life.

Then in a very surprised voice she exclaimed, "That's right! I only have headaches when he is with me or when I am in our house....I went to Rochester once and stayed a whole month so they could study my headaches, but Jim wasn't with me and I didn't have a headache the whole time." She asserted that in the nearly twenty years of being with her husband she had not noticed that particular pattern to the headaches.

After the death of the wicked ruler, it was explained to her that she had a choice. Because of her great cruelties she would have to return many times to painful experiences to expiate them. An alternative choice would be to have the evil burned away in a purifying fire.

She chose the fire, describing it as very much like the hell we were taught about in Sunday School except that it wasn't permanent. "It only feels permanent while you are there," she said.

Following this "hell" experience, she never again returned to her evil ways. She did experience a large number of difficult lives later. Each of these lives contained a lesson or lessons — opportunities for growth in awareness. In some of them she learned. Some seemed to be more recess than learning.

I worked with Anne intermittently over a period of about six years. The headaches left completely. She evolved as a balanced, insightful caring person who through a highly developed psychic sensitivity has helped hundreds of people.

As she related her feeling of being free, of being relieved of a great burden through reviewing her many past lives, of knowing that the choices both in the past and present were her own, I felt a quiet joy that I had succeeded in helping not only Anne, but through her so many others.

I am including a portion of a transcript which includes bits of the final days of the black priestess, Antonius and Marija, three that were of utmost importance in our six years of work.

A. A.   I'm about to die. I have my slave open my ring and pour the poison into the cup. I raised it. It is very difficult to drink it.

Dr. H.   Detach yourself and describe what's happening. Step aside and watch.

A. A.   It's paralysis. It attacks the neck first, the right arm. The muscles twitch and the stomach contracts. Then she just slumped over. It was not a very gruesome death. It was rather passive.

Dr. H.   Then what happened to the body?

A. A.   I had oil. I had given orders that the oil be spread all the way round my room and set fire. This is what's happening now.

Dr. H.   You are able to see this?

A. A.   Yes.

Dr. H.   What are your thoughts and feelings now that you are out of your body?

A. A.   Not good.

Dr. H.   What about it isn't good?

A. A.   I just feel very sad. I can't quite understand it yet. I don't understand why I should feel this way. I don't feel a bit good about it.

Dr. H.   Go on. Describe anything that you are experiencing after leaving this body.

A. A.   I hung around there for quite a while. I couldn't get away. The attachment was too great. It was days before I could get away from there. The body was charred. There wasn't much left of it. I'm just looking and I feel sort of lost.

Dr. H.   Go forward until a change has occurred in what you are experiencing. What happens next?

A. A.   I ascended.

Dr. H.   Do you know where you ascended to?

A. A.   The door was locked. I recognized this path—I had been here before, but this time the door was locked. I couldn't get through.

Dr. H.   What did you do? Where did you go?

A. A.   They pointed down there.

Dr. H.   Did you go down there?

A. A.   I had to go down there.

Dr. H.   What is it like down there?

A. A.   Evil, dirty.

Dr. H.   Did you recognize that you had brought yourself there? Were there regrets then for your evil life?

A. A.   Terrible — terrible!

Dr. H.   How long did you have to stay there?

A. A.   Years. Many many years.

Dr. H.   Tell me what it was like.

A. A.   I knew there were others there. I could hear them moaning. I couldn't see them. All I could see were these monsters around me that I had created. I tried to abolish them with my magic but it didn't work. They just laughed at me. I tried calling up the flame to destroy them. It didn't work. There's one monster right in front of me. Hideous — it was one I had created. I called him the dweller. I call up the flame. He walks right through it. Nothing works here. I realize it now. I realize that I will just have to stay here.

Dr. H.   Are you aware of any change that has to occur before you can leave this place?

A. A.   Something has to take place in my heart. A change has to take place within me.

Dr. H.   Do you know what that change is?

A. A.   It looks like the unfolding of a flower. It looks like petals that I have to open up.

Dr. H.   As you look at this unopened flower, how does it appear to you?

A. A.   It looks like a flower that has been very beautiful, but has been neglected and no water given it. It is just limp and dry. But with proper care it would flower forth and be beautiful again.

Dr. H.   Go forward in time to when this begins to be beautiful again.

A. A.   It's very slow — so slow. I feel as though I am lifted up and am dropping an outer body or skin that was very heavy and very course. Now it has been refined. The texture is different. There is an airy feeling as the flower opens up more and more.

Dr. H.   Are you still surrounded by the evil beings?

A. A.   Not so much. I know that they are there, but I realize that they can't hurt me now.

Dr. H.   Go on and tell any other changes that contribute to this greater feeling of purity and lightness.

A. A.   I need to meditate and learn to pray.

Dr. H.   Even though you have no physical body?

A. A.   I just have awareness of my consciousness. I just don't feel a body. Suddenly there is this ray of beautiful, beautiful sunlight. It touches me.

Dr. H.   How does this effect you?

A. A.   It attracts my attention and I look up — like a new day. I reach out and someone takes my hand. As they take my hand I float up out of the evil area and up into space.

Dr. H.   What is your next experience?

A. A.   Little cherubs again. (Anne mentioned cherubs around her several times as she was between one death and the next birth.)

Dr. H.   O.K. Go through the experience of the cherubs. What happens next?

A. A.   I'm in the valley again. I look around. More meditation.

Dr. H.   Is there any special meaning or significance to your valley? Does it have anything to do with your acquiring a new body?

A. A.   The only thing I get is that this is the place where you learn to combine the physical with the spiritual.

Dr. H.   Do you go to the valley after your new body has

been conceived?

A. A.   Yes.

Dr. H.   And while you are in the valley, your body is being formed? Is that right?

A. A.   Right.

Dr. H.   You mentioned once before that when you entered the valley you felt very small and that you became larger and more complete as you progressed through the valley. Go on and describe any of the details of the valley experience that you may have omitted as we went over this before.

A. A.   It seems as though I understand all nature here. It seems as though I can communicate with them — the trees, the flowers, the grass. I seem to be a part of them. I seem to be this sphere that encompasses everything. I'm just one with them and they're one with me. As I move toward the far end of the valley, I understand these things more and I feel more and more complete until I'm finally let out.

Dr. H.   And when you are let out, what is that called?

A. A.   Birth.

Dr. H.   Then proceed on to the birth of the next body after the life you have just described. What's happening?

A. A.   I'm looking to see where I am going to be born. There it is. I'm being born.

Dr. H.   Are you a male or female baby?

A. A.   Male.

Dr. H.   Now go on to the next major event in the life of this baby.

A. A.   I'm the Roman, Antonius.

Dr. H.   You've gone over this several times, but if

there is anything else you need to say about your life as Antonius at the count of three you'll be there. 1,2,3. What's happening now?

A. A.   I am employed by Julius Caesar. In fact I lived there with him. I was trained as an athlete.

Dr. H.   Did you like this life?

A. A.   Yes, very much. There was none of the magic or ritual. It was all physical.

Dr. H.   What was the reason for your coming into this life?

A. A.   To be of service.

Dr. H.   Tell anything else you need to say about the life of Antonius.

A. A.   I did the right thing by not joining the ones who wanted to kill him.

Dr. H.   Were there any wrong things you did as Antonius? Did you make any mistakes?

A. A.   I didn't protect him well enough. This was one of my jobs—to protect him and I didn't. I feel that there was something I could have done to prevent it.

Dr. H.   Was there anything you did as Antonius that you ought not to have done?

A. A.   No. Ask me what happened to the man who ordered me dragged behind the chariot.

Dr. H.   Oh yes. What happened to "Fancy Pants"?

A. A.   He was killed in some way. He didn't make out too well after I died—after he had me put to death. All that I know is that he was acting under orders.

Dr. H.   Have you talked about these things enough that your headaches can be absolutely dispensed with and be no more?

A. A.   Yes. They're gone.

Dr. H.   Then go on to any later important event. You
          have left the body of Antonius. Go to any other
          event that will help you understand yourself,
          Anne, in 1966. (Here Anne began beautiful
          rythmic gestures with her hands.) What is your
          name?

A. A.   Marija. I'm a temple dancer in Siam. This is my
          favorite, favorite life. I could do anything I
          wanted to do. The dances included some of the
          same symbols I used for the magic before, but
          they're not being used for that now. Just for
          adoration.

Dr. H.   Is there any particular reason that you need to
          talk about this life, or are you just enjoying it?

A. A.   I enjoy it.

Anne went on to describe a life in France that was also
pleasant and to which she referred to as a "big recess."

After we had eliminated the stored emotions connected
with the many lives she reviewed, she was able to be so
psychically sensitive to other people, that she became most
adept as a counsellor. She seemed to have the ability to so accurately tune in to another person that she would have both
the bodily sensations and the memory of that other person.

In the years we worked together she had made a tremendous change from the housewife with daily severe migraine
headaches to a comfortable, healthy, gifted helper of hundreds of others.

It has been a joyous experience for me to have played a
part in this change.

Chapter 6

BIRTH AND DEATH

"It is as natural to man to die, as to be born; and to the little infant, perhaps one is as painful as the other."
                                                    Francis Bacon

Among my records there are a great number and variety of birth and death experiences. From these reports it is easy to think of death as holding fewer terrors than birth. This is surprising in that we are accustomed to thinking that death is the tragic event and birth the joyous one.

Death has come to my patients in many forms; some brutal and gruesome, some suicides, some a peaceful dying during sleep. Prior deaths have left scars that made themselves felt in present life patterns and reactions as well as attitudes.

One girl found the source of her severe allergy to cats in an attack by a tiger. Then, a male warrior and scout, encountered a tiger on a path, almost outwitted him, but made one mistake, was attacked, and devoured by the animal. She/he then told of watching the tiger eat the body from the level of the treetops. After she was guided through the attack incident four times—each repetition characterized by ever diminishing intensity of reaction—the cat allergy was gone.

Steve, a young man with exaggerated intolerance to cold weather found three former lives in which death was related to extreme cold.

A phobia for sharp objects was relieved after the patient relived her former death as a result of falling on a pitchfork.

A friend, Bill, experienced a former life as a tubercular alcoholic who hemorrhaged and died in the snow one night as he staggered home drunkenly from the tavern. I suggested to him when the death agonies began that he go forward until he had left the body, in order to be spared the discomfort of the

68

death struggle. He refused and said that he had to go through this so that he would never repeat the pattern.

Mark, once a palace guard in Spain succumbed to the thrust of a Moorish sword when the Moors invaded Spain.

Mildred, fearful of falling from high places found the fear to have originated when she was thrown from a cliff as a result of her being discovered to be a spy in the time of Cyrus the Great.

Stella died of dysentery from drinking contaminated milk. In the present life the milk intolerance has persisted.

Jack as a Montana Indian died of starvation during a severe winter.

Sande was relieved of her spider phobia after going over a time when she was killed by a poisonous bite of a huge spider.

Jay found the source of his stuttering and inability to talk to or relate to women of his own generation in a past experience of being hanged in Placerville, Ca. (Also known as Hangtown) after being caught in bed with another man's wife.

Dean just became tired and died in his sleep.

All of these people were able to relate reactions in the present life to former experiences. When the old emotions were uncovered, worked through cathartically, they were no longer a problem in the present life. None of my patients expressed any feeling that death was something to dread, to avoid at all costs. Most seemed to be relieved.

Birth was an entirely different matter. Only a few found birth to be something they eagerly looked forward to. The more common reaction was regret, reluctance or even refusal.

One of the rare eager ones was Patricia, who was so eager that she pushed others aside and rushed in mistakenly getting in the wrong family.

Ethel, when asked why she had chosen her family, replied, "The body was available." Further questioning obtained the same response. When she heard her tape recording she responded with, "Next time I am going to be more discriminating."

Annie, when reliving her birth, realized that her mother had never wanted her. Further examination showed her that her mother was not just rejecting her (as she had always felt) but had not wanted any baby. When she realized that no one could have pleased her mother, she was able to see her mother in a new light and relate to her without the old guilt and striving to please. She was able to discontinue the futile effort which had been her lifelong pattern.

Letitia, when asked to tell what was being said at the time of her birth replied, "I hear somebody yelling 'Go get the doctor'." She later learned that her birth was a complete surprise to her mother, who had had both fallopian tubes surgically removed seven years earlier. Her birth had occurred early one morning. Her mother had felt a few cramps and the baby had gone "plop" on the floor. Mother had, indeed, shouted, "Go get the doctor!" This had not previously been told Letitia.

Sande told of being born at home and that her grandmother had been present. She was able to describe the grandmother's appearance and her actions. She also noted that her mother's hair was much lighter than she knew it to be from her usual memory. She was able to verify these details. Her grandmother had been present at her birth, but had died when Sande was three months old. Mother's hair had been lighter also at the time of Sande's birth.

Carol came to me because she had always felt confused about who her mother was. She felt more the daughter of a sister than of the one who was in the mother role. She regressed back to before birth and saw that both her "mother" and her "sister" were expecting at the same time. The "mother's" baby was born first. She entered that body, which was frail and weak. Three days later the "sister's" baby was born, at which time the first baby died. Carol, now free, entered the body of the "sister's" baby. The sister, very young and in the process of being divorced, agreed that it would be best if folks were told that her baby had died and that the mother (grandmother) should raise the living baby as her own. When Carol realized that she had been both babies, and that both her "sister" and her "mother" were her mothers, the confusion was resolved and ceased to trouble her.

The most interesting birth report—and the most amusing—was lived with vivid reality in January of 1982. Here a girl who wore the name of Liddy was kidnapped and choked

70

to death in Chicago. The transcript of this tape follows. Unfortunately written words fall far short of giving the true impression. Only the hearing of the tape with it's extremes of vocal expression, or still better, being present to watch her expressions, gestures and movements can depict the scene accurately.

D. M.   He took a silk scarf and put it around my neck and choked me.

Dr. H.   Look back at your life as Liddy and tell me about her.

D. M.   She was a very smart girl—very smart. I don't want to go down there anymore. I don't want to go back again.

Dr. H.   It's nice not having a body for a while isn't it?

D. M.   I don't ever want a body again.

Dr. H.   It's 1940 when you left the body of Liddy. So in 1940 you don't have a body. Let's go forward now. It's 1941. Do you have a body in 1941?

D. M.   (Petulantly.) No.

Dr. H.   Are you still feeling that you don't want to go back again?

D. M.   I don't ever want to go again. I don't ever, I don't ever, I don't ever.

Dr. H.   Now it's 1942.

D. M.   No! I don't want to go back. Don't make me go back.

Dr. H.   1943.

D. M.   No! I don't want to!

Dr. H.   1944, 1945, 1946, 1947.

D. M.   I'm not going back.

Dr. H.   1948.

D. M.   I don't want to go back!

Dr. H.   1949. . .(pause). . . 1950. (A very displeased expression came over her face, and she appeared to be trying to draw away from something.) How are you feeling about having a body in 1950? Would you like to have a body in 1950? (Gestures of displeasure.) What's happening? What are you experiencing? It's 1950.

D. M.   (Disgustedly.) I've got a body!

Dr. H.   Tell me about it.

D. M.   No, (Almost shouting.) No, I don't want to be here!

Dr. H.   Tell me about the body you have in 1950.

D. M.   I'm a baby.

Dr. H.   Tell me about. . . .

D. M.   (Interrupting.) No, I don't want to. I'm not going to live very long — not long at all.

Dr. H.   How long?

D. M.   Two.

Dr. H.   Now it's 1951. How old are you in 1951?

D. M.   One.

Dr. H.   So in 1952 you are two. Tell me about the end of that life. How do you feel about having a body now that you are two years old?

D. M.   I just don't WANT ONE!

Dr. H.   Tell me about it. What are you going to do about it if you don't like having a body?

D. M.   I'm going to leave.

Dr. H.   Are you a baby girl or baby boy?

D. M.   A boy!!!

Dr. H.   What's your name?

D. M.   I don't care! I'm leaving.

Dr. H.   O.K. How are you leaving? Go to the time you are leaving and tell me how you do it.

D. M.   There's some nice junk in the cupboard that Mommy set down, so I'm just going to eat it and die and go away.

Dr. H.   Do you eat it and die?

D. M.   Yes. I'm gone.

Dr. H.   Do you feel better now?

D. M.   Yes.

Dr. H.   In 1952 you got rid of that body. It's now 1953. How do you feel about having a body in 1953?

D. M.   I don't want another body!

Dr. H.   1954. What happens? Do you have a body in 1954?

D. M.   No!

Dr. H.   1955. Do you have a body?

D. M.   No.

Dr. H.   1956?

D. M.   NO! I don't want to go back.

Dr. H.   Is someone telling you that you need to go back?

D. M.   I've got to go back. There's just no end. They're just not going to leave me alone 'til I do.

Dr. H.   Who is not going to leave you alone until you go back?

D. M.   They just keep telling me that I'm not going to get anywhere sitting around here. Why can't God just say, "O.K. You don't have to go back, Honey"? He just keeps pointing his finger and saying, "You gotta learn!" I don't wanta learn. I don't want to go back!

Dr. H.   1956. What's happening in 1956?

D. M.   He says to make up my mind.

Dr. H.   Are you making up your mind?

D. M.   I don't *want* to go back!

Dr. H.   What do you decide?

D. M.   I decided to go talk to him again.

Dr. H.   O.K. Go talk to him again. What does he say?

D. M.   I DON'T WANT TO GO BACK!! I just don't understand why you're doing this to me.

Dr. H.   What is said to you?

D. M.   That I've just got to go. There's just no other answer. He's not going to let me sit around here no longer.

Dr. H.   So, you're being kicked out?

D. M.   Yes.

Dr. H.   Where are you going if you can't sit around there any longer?

D. M.   (Despondently.) I don't know.

Dr. H.   The time is getting shorter and shorter. It's about time for you to go back again. Where are you going to?

D. M.   Just let me sit on my cloud and look down. (She leans forward in the chair and looks toward the floor.)

Dr. H.   Fine, sit on your cloud and look. See if you can find a good place to go.

D. M.   There are no good places to go.

Dr. H.   Is there a place that you think you can tolerate?

D. M.   (Pointing to the right.) There's a place over there.

Dr. H.   What is it like?

D. M.   Very nice. Very cozy. A lot of love.

Dr. H.   What kind of family would you have if you go there?

D. M.   Very kind.

Dr. H.   Are there already children there?

D. M.   Yeah. Two.

Dr. H.   If you go there will you be a girl or a boy?

D. M.   (Impatiently.) I don't know yet.

Dr. H.   Let's look to see if there are other places for you to go that you think you could stand. Do you see any others?

D. M.   (Pointing forward.) There's one over there.

Dr. H.   Tell me about the family over here.

D. M.   They look very happy.

Dr. H.   Do they have any children?

D. M.   Nope.

Dr. H.   So if you go there you will be the first one?

D. M.   Yeah. (Pleasurably.)

Dr. H.   Will you be a boy or girl if you go here? Or do you know?

D. M.   I'm not concerned with that. If I've got to go back, I don't care how I go back.

Dr. H.   The time is getting shorter. Which one of these places are you going to choose? Or are you still looking for another one?

D. M.   Well, there's one over there (Pointing to the left.) They've got five kids. I don't think I'd like that.

Dr. H.   Are there any other choices that you have?

D. M.   Nope.

Dr. H.   So you have three choices. One, you would be the third child. In the next one, you would be the first child. And in the last one you would be the sixth child. Which one do you think you are going to choose.

D. M.   (Sullenly.) I don't know.

Dr. H.   It's getting time for you to choose. You must make up your mind. If you are going back it will have to be in one of these families.

D. M.   Well . . . . .

Dr. H.   Do you know any of these people? Are they people you have know before or are they strangers?

D. M.   These two people over here I know (right). And these two people over here I know(front). I know both of these couples.

Dr. H.   What do you know about the ones who don't have any children yet?

D. M.   They're young. Father is outgoing. He's a nice guy. He's always had it hard. He bitches a lot. She's very nice. Very small, very softspoken. She does anything he wants her to. She's very sad and lonely.

Dr. H.   Is that the one you choose?

D. M.   Yeah.

Dr. H.   Are they expecting a child yet?

D. M.   Yep. . . . I don't want to go back!

Dr. H.   Are you going to be their child?

D. M.   Pfffft.

Dr. H.   How do you feel about it. Say anything you want to.

D. M.   I don't want to go back, and I don't want to be stuck with this family so I have to raise them.

Dr. H.   Do you go to them?

D. M.   Yes.

Dr. H.   Go to the time you have just been born. You have a body again. How do you feel about it.

D. M.   (Very disgustedly.) Whoopee. I don't want to be here!

Dr. H.   What do you do about it?

D. M.   Can't die. He'll just kick me back down here again as soon as I get back up there. He's already told me that.

Dr. H.   You tried that didn't you?

D. M.   Curly hair no less. No freak has curly hair. Nobody. I feel like spitting in the Doc's face. (Spit.)

Dr. H.   Now leave this scene. You are growing up. Come forward all the way to January 22, 1982. You're grown up now and it's time to wake up.

The case of another most reluctant birth is selected from a tape recording made by another hypnotist.

This subject had described a most unsatisfactory life in which he had an unusual and hated name and a totally dominating mother. He told of his death in Denver in 1912 shortly after an unsuccessful suicide attempt.

L. R.   They're just pulling the sheet up. He's gone. His wife felt sorry for him because he wasn't a man. He didn't know what else to do with himself . .

W. L.   What are you doing now?

L. R.   I'm outside now, just trying to understand. Oh, that explains why I'm so afraid of women . . . .

W. L.   It's now 1913...1913

L. R.   That's funny. In 1913, I can see a little girl. Her name is Mary Anne. She's going to have a brother.

W. L.   Are you going to be that brother?

L. R.   Yeah. That's the funniest thing. She's patting her mother's stomach. She says, "That's my brother in there." I'm in there, but I'm outside too.

W. L.   You want to be born?

L. R.   If she's going to be my sister, I guess I want to be born. She's such a nice girl. . I just decided that I want to be her brother. If she wants to have a brother, I want to be that brother. This is silly. Why should I want to be her brother?

W. L.   You are going to be born. All is well. Describe your birth.

L. R.   I'm up in the air watching.

W. L.   You're watching yourself being born?

L. R.   I see a funny looking little head coming out sideways. He's twisting it sideways.

W. L.   What else is happening?

L. R.   I don't know. It may not happen.

W. L.   What may not happen.

L. R.   I may not be born.

W. L.   Describe everything.

L. R.   I hear somebody screaming. It's all over and she's still screaming. Why doesn't she just relax?

W. L.   Can you help her in any way?

L. R.   I'm separated from her now. The doctor is cleaning me up. I'm a mess. He's drawing something away from my face and I'm breathing.

W. L.   Did the doctor spank you?

L. R.   No, he didn't spank me. He just held me in his hand and I started breathing.

W. L.   When you started breathing were you aware any more of who you were before, or who you are going to be?

L. R.   There's some kind of trouble. I don't want to go in there.

W. L.   Where?

L. R.   In that body — that baby. It's just trouble all over again. Every time you go through this it's just the same thing over and over and over.

W. L.   You came to learn something.

L. R.   What can you learn? People are stupid and they don't get any smarter. No one likes you and they give you a funny name and you end up in the hospital, and it's all over, and then I have to face it again. I don't want to do it almost. I feel like I have to, but I don't want to do it . . . . . . But if I don't he won't live. What a choice! (Pause.) . . Seems like everything is frozen. Nobody's moving. Everything stops while I am making up my mind. It's a big job. (Pause.) To get the courage to do it again. Why do it? It doesn't make any sense. You just go through it and through it and through it . . . . . If I could just learn something!

W. L.   What are they naming the baby?

L. R.   They're naming him Leonard Robert. (Long pause.) I'm not there yet. I don't know if I want to. I don't know if I want to do it. If I just thought there was any possibility of making this little baby happy, I would. But that baby — what chance has he got more than anybody else?

W. L.   You have to be born.

L. R.   I've got to do something. I can't just sit here. If I don't who will? Maybe somebody else will do it. I don't see anybody else around.

W. L.   Going in . . . . . (Pause.) One year old now.

79

L. R.   No, don't rush me. Just don't rush me. I'm just going in — going in. I'm just in. Let me rest for a minute. I hope it will work out. What chance does he have to learn something? This poor little baby — he didn't do anything to anybody. What can I do to help him better? What can I do to help him be better? To learn something? To not just muddle through? I don't know. I'm just a baby. I guess I'll have to give up. I'm just a baby and that's all there is to it. I had no choice to stay out there. I can't just stay out there. I want to go back with the brownies — the little people.

These examples of births and deaths are only a few of the many my patients and trainees have contributed.

Although the deaths were often violent and left lingering emotional problems, the feeling immediately after death was of freedom and few regrets.

Birth, in contrast, required the assumption of difficult or unpleasant limitations and responsibilities.

Additional data could clarify whether our traditional views of birth as a happy event and death as a sad one are correct. My cases suggest that the reverse view is the true one.

Chapter 7

THE HYPNOTISM CONTROVERSY

"Controversy is wretched when it is only an attempt to prove another wrong—It destroys humble enquiry after truth and throws all our energies into an attempt to prove ourselves right—a spirit in which no man gets at truth"   F. W. Robertson

It is not possible to discuss hypnosis without also discussing controversy. There is and seemingly always has been disagreement about the method, the desirability and the alleged dangers of the use of hypnotism.

Again and again hypnotism has sunk almost into oblivion, only to be revived by courageous pioneers who have braved the onslaught of criticism and opposition.

The hypnotist has been depicted as a powerful and usually evil person who controlled the will of others.

So soiled became the reputation of hypnosis that only the most courageous would risk their reputations to come near enough to test the facts for themselves.

Hypnotism has been used since antiquity. Witch doctors, medicine men of primitive tribes and early religious leaders have used hypnosis in various forms to heal the sick.

Perhaps the oldest record of hypnosis is from the Ebers Papyrus which is over 3000 years old. This papyrus relates how techniques closely approximating those used today were used by ancient Egyptians.

Early medical records describe healings in the Temple of Aesculapius in ancient Greece. Here suffering people were placed in a state of sleep—sometimes for days—until they recovered from their illnesses.

In spite of its great age, hypnotism has not found easy acceptance. The entire history of hypnotism has been frought with controversy and conflict.

From the days of Frans Anton Mesmer, the man who is given most credit for promoting and developing this altered state of consciousness, the polarization has been intense, sometimes brutal and often costly for practitioners or participants.

Mesmer, who studied for the priesthood, then law and finally medicine, was intrigued by reports of a priest in the south of France who had gained a high reputation as a healer of the afflicted.

The story is told of how Mesmer visited the priest (who had the unusual name of Father Hell) and watched the priest as he ministered to the suffering. As the ill ones were brought before Father Hell, the priest would stroke their bodies. They would appear to fall into a trance state. When they awakened, they appeared to be free of their illness — totally relieved of their afflictions. Many were suffering from illnesses of obvious emotional or nervous origins. There were also some with physical illnesses.

Mesmer reasoned that there must be some form of energy passing from the hands of the priest to evoke the healing. He thought of this energy as magnetism and called it animal magnetism. He ventured to reproduce the actions of Father Hell and was successful in allaying much illness himself.

Then he began using actual magnets in treating others. Mesmer's first patient to be treated with magnets came to him in July, 1774. She suffered from many disabilities — fainting, vomiting, convulsions, delirium, earaches, toothaches and many others. She had seen many doctors with her many complaints. She was pronounced incurable and was expected to die very soon.

Mesmer placed his newly designed magnets on her legs and stomach, repeating the treatments every few days. Within a few weeks the woman had recovered completely. This and other similar cases spread Mesmer's fame. Soon Mesmer's name was well known everywhere. Hundreds of people began seeking his help for their ills.

These were often men and women from high society or with important positions in government or business — people of great influence. Mesmer's fame spread through European society. He was soon besieged by great numbers of people seeking his help. To accommodate them all he devised various kinds of equipment and "magnetized" many common objects.

His most famous creation was the Baquet—a big oaken tub. Into the tub went iron filings, powdered glass, carefully arranged bottles, water and iron rods. Patients would sit around the Baquet holding the rods to receive the beneficial effects of the magnetism.

Mesmer's operation was investigated by a commission of the Royal Academy of Science and the Faculty of Medicine in Vienna. Their report was so critical that Mesmer was soon thereafter expelled from the medical fraternity, this in spite of numerous reports from Mesmer's patients that they had been cured by the methods. He soon left Vienna under great pressure, going first to Paris and then to Spa, Belgium.

By this time he had stopped using magnetized objects and the Baquet. Instead he stroked the patients with his fingers to induce a trance state. In Spa, he performed many cures. Some were near miraculous, including successes in treating the mentally ill.

After a period of time he felt confident enough to return to Paris. Again he gained fame and again he met opposition. Again he was investigated by a Commission.

The report of the commission concluded that the treatment "might be harmful", and that his methods were "unwholesome."

The established medical society ridiculed Mesmer and refused to investigate the phenomena in any real way. Mesmerism and animal magnetism, the name he had used, were dead.

However, just as the commission was preparing the condemning report on Mesmer, the Marquis de Puysegur published a paper telling of his practice of animal magnetism on his peasant tenants. He was so successful he was looked upon as a saint. So many came for help that he could not tend them all. To accommodate as many as possible, he magnetized some ropes and hung them from a tree in the village square. People would come, sit on the stone benches, wrapping the magnetized roped around themselves to get some magnetism for easing their pain and illness.

It was at this place that he observed a very strange happening. A young boy named Victor, who sat among the others appeared to fall asleep. He remained there for such a long time that the Marquis told him to untie himself and get up. Without opening his eyes the boy obeyed. Then he walked across the park, his eyes still closed. This intrigued the Marquis, who began experimenting with Victor. The boy had the ability to fall into a deep sleep or trance at his command, and to obey any order given him. Upon awakening from the trance he had total amnesia for what had transpired. The Marquis gave the name "somnambulism" or sleep walking to this phenomenon.

In spite of the results, opposition persisted. The Commission of 1784 included in its report the statement that Mesmer's cures were not due to magnetism, but to imagination. In response to this, one of Mesmer's pupils, Charles d'Eslon said, "If the medicine of imagination is best, why should we not practice the medicine of imagination?"

Neither Mesmer nor dePuysegur gained acclaim for their discoveries. They were branded as heretics to scientific thought. Mesmer, defeated, went into lonely retirement. He died in Switzerland in 1815 without honor or even recognition for his great contribution. His name had become a symbol of derision and of evil.

The idea, the fact, the remarkable benefits of hypnotism, mesmerism, somnambulism could not however, be defeated. Always a courageous few continued to study and to use hypnotism.

The greatest interest developed in France, where in 1864 a Nancy physician, Ambroise Leibault began to use hypnosis. His cures were remarkable. His success led to widespread fame. The poor, whom he treated without charge revered him as a saint.

Another Nancy physician, Hippolite Bernheim, bitterly denounced Leibault in a medical article. However, when Leibault cured a man whom Bernheim had unsuccessfully treated for six years, Bernheim was pursuaded to reexamine his attitude. Bernheim first observed Leibault and then began to use hypnosis in his own clinic. He kept very careful records of more than 5,000 successfully treated patients. He helped keep medical hypnosis alive, and nurtured the slowly growing interest in the therapy.

During this time, Dr. Jean Martin Charcot was becoming

the most popular and admired physician in all of France, particularly for his success in treating the mentally ill. He had become head of the School of Salpetriere and in 1879, after learning about hypnosis and recognizing its value in treating the mentally ill, he authorized the use of hypnosis with hysterical patients and kept careful notes of its use and of its benefits.

Charcot contributed much to medical thinking regarding hypnosis. He classified hypnosis into three stages: lethergy, represented by physical relaxation; catalepsy, during which the limbs could be placed in any position and would remain; and somnambulism or deepest state during which subjects could talk, walk or become anesthetized. He lectured on hypnosis. His audiences, both lay and professional, filled the lecture halls. Charcot's great reputation enabled him to have a paper on hypnosis accepted by the Academy of Science, (without enthusiasm.)

Another commission was appointed, which did not render its report until nine years later. The matter was forgotten.

An obscure young physician from Vienna came to Paris to listen to the great Charcot and became impressed with his abilities and his successes. He, a slight scholarly Austrian, Sigmund Freud, had first become acquainted with hypnosis by watching Dr. Breuer, of Vienna, use hypnosis in treating a hysterical woman, Anna O. When Anna O. was hypnotized and questioned she had related to Dr. Breuer details of great intimacy regarding her sexual life. When these incidents were recalled and relived, her tensions and physical symptoms were relieved. The concept that the reviewing or reliving of long-repressed memories of painful experiences could relieve the mind and body of present pains, sowed the seeds that later became psychoanalysis.

Freud also studied with Leibault at Nancy, and with Bernheim. Then he returned to Vienna and began using hypnosis, "The talking cure," with his patients. So many of his patients related their symptoms to sexual problems that Freud was led to believe that all problems originated in sexual responses. His contribution to the understanding of human sexuality has been great. It is unfortunate that he gave almost no attention to the other numerous facets of man's mind.

Among others who contributed greatly was Chevelier Barbarin, who founded a school in Lyons, France; M. Deleuse, who in 1813 published a book, A Critical History of Animal Magnetism, which stated that anyone could learn to be a magnetizer if they desired to help others.

Of the many doctors who tried hypnotism, some of them discarded it as imagination of the patient. A few felt that there was some value in it, but used it rarely. A still smaller number continued to work earnestly with it.

In 1821, the first surgery was performed on a patient in a deep somnambulistic trance. About this same time the magnetizing of epileptics was authorized at Salpetriere, the first and most famous mental institution in France.

The mesmerism controversy spread to England, where members of high society began to seek magnetic treatments as word-of-mouth information spread concerning its use by certain doctors. Soon many teachers and practitioners of mesmerism developed.

An American, Benjamin Perkins, who lived in England, acquired a license for an invention to produce magnetic healing. This consisted of small pieces of metal which he claimed were capable of attracting the illness out of the body.

His success came to an end when someone painted some pieces of wood to resemble the metal "tractors" and substituted them for the metal. Strangely, the wood was able to produce the same cures as the metal, but Perkins was disgraced.

One of the great pioneers in the use of Mesmerism in England was Dr. John Elliotson, perfector of the stethoscope. He began using hypnotism in treating the mentally disturbed. His fellow doctors opposed him with increasing energy. In 1837, he was prohibited from using hypnosis in London Hospital. Later, when he persisted in using hypnosis, he was called a "madman" and prohibited from lecturing before the medical society.

Here and there were small forward movements toward acceptance and recognition of hypnosis as a useful medical modality. The violent attacks delayed, but did not destroy mesmerism. A Mesmeric Infirmary was established in London. Mesmeric Institutes were founded in Edinburgh, Dublin and Exeter. A Dr. Parker used mesmerism regularly for surgical operations, performing more than two hundred surgeries under hypnoanesthesia, in spite of the attacks on him.

In 1842 in Nottinghamshire, a Dr. Ward removed a tumor from a man's thigh with only hypnosis for anesthetic. The perfect success of the operation did not protect Dr. Ward's reputation. He was viciously attacked. One doctor claimed that Dr. Ward had simply trained the patient to fake comfort and lie still in spite of pain. Other doctors supported the idea that pain was natural and ought to be suffered when a surgeon cut.

The most outstanding use of hypnosis in the last century was by James Esdaile, a doctor for the East India Company. He had read about mesmerism in the *Zoist*, a magazine published by Elliotson. He first tried mesmerism out on a convict he was treating. To his astonishment, the convict fell quickly into a deep trance. Esdaile subsequently performed several hundred surgical operations using only mesmerism as anesthetic. Most of the operations were for a condition so dangerous that many physicians refused to accept the cases. This was for the removal of a scrotal tumor — a common ailment in India at that time. For this operation the usual mortality rate was 50%. Esdaile's mortality rate was about 5% in the more than 200 such surgeries he performed with no anesthetic except hypnosis. As his workload increased, he trained hospital attendants to do the mesmerizing. He then had more time to perform the surgeries.

Success or not, neither the Indian nor the English medical societies were impressed. Their attack continued upon mesmerism and upon all who tried to use or defend it. Esdaile was ridiculed, belittled and demeaned. He was expelled from the British Medical Society.

His success was explained away with the claims that low-caste patients loved operations, and were just pretending not to have pain in order to get the operations and to please Esdaile.

Similar criticism and opposition met Dr. James Braid, of Scotland, The French Journal of Mental Science called his work Braidism's Artificial Insanity. He continued to use the techniques of hypnosis, and to experience growing success.

He was influential in popularizing the terms hypnosis and hypnotism—from the Greek, *Hypnos*, meaning sleep.

In spite of the success of those doctors using hypnosis, the medical profession almost unanimously ignored this modality. Only a rare and courageous physician dared risk his reputation with its use.

Hypnosis was kept alive largely by stage magicians, fakers and charlatans, who at the same time perpetuated the taint on the word. Hypnosis has continued to be poorly understood or misunderstood because of the distortions and misrepresentations in literature, drama, film and television.

The result is that physicians are still being taught and are conducting their office practices with almost purely materialistic points of view—that we are only a physical body. What little thought that is given to the mind is concerned with physiological changes possible through the use of chemicals.

Little thought has been given to the possibility that humanness is more than a physical body whose brain somehow secretes what is called "mind."

The proper use of hypnosis can demonstrate that we are indeed more than just physical—that we are truly an immortal soul or spirit clothed in and operating through a physical body.

Few doctors, psychiatrists or psychologists will professionally admit that there is a soul or spirit. Many will concede that there might be a "something" which we do not as yet understand, but are hesitant either to discuss or investigate the possibility of a soul. Since it is not understood, it is almost totally ignored.

This position is both unrealistic and dishonest. If doctors were to limit their treatment to only those things fully understood, few therapies would be used. Actually we have very limited understanding of why or how anyone becomes sick, or why or how they become well again. We have only the slightest idea of the purpose of illness in the experience of man, or whether illness has a meaning.

Neither the God of the church nor the newer God of science that we have looked to for solutions have been able to fill our plea to "Deliver us from evil."

We need to reexamine and rethink the questions as to

what man *is*, his purpose and his destiny. Neither the church God nor the science God has adequately provided us with the "daily bread" so needful for our continued harmonious existence.

We can now, I believe, take the materialism of science and the spirituality of religion and blend them together. This can result in a new substance with which we can shape the future.

Hypnosis can bring healing in an area where these two facets link together naturally. It already partakes of both worlds, and by its use both worlds can become better understood.

As hypnosis is gradually coming into wider acceptance and use by physicians, dentists, psychologists, law enforcement workers, teachers, personal counsellors and researchers, the taint is fading. There is also a growing number of hypnotechnicians who are working in conjunction with physicians and psychologists. Florida and California have given official recognition to this professional group.

In 1958 the American Medical Association for the first time gave official sanction to the use of hypnosis by physicians. Hypnosis has now a measure of respectability, but it still has not been able to fully shed the cloud of suspicion and avoidance. This has limited its use to a few and rendered it unavailable to all but a very small percentage of the ailing public.

Chapter 8

DISPELLING THE MYTHS

"Error of theory or doctrine are not so much false statements as partial statements. — —Half a truth received, while the corresponding half is unknown or rejected, is a partial falsehood." Tryon Edwards.

From Mesmer to Freud, many sincere and dedicated men lost their professional standing, and some even their fortunes because they dared to practice hypnosis, or to support approvingly its practice by others.

Medical knowledge is developed with deadly slowness. Whenever a new idea appears to contradict accepted ideas and practices, the movement is so slow it at times appears to be backward instead of forward. It is comfortable to feel that our present ideas and understanding contains the truth. It is uncomfortable to have to admit that we may be inadequately trained or knowledgeable.

We are inclined to attack anything which would require us to change our ideas. Hypnosis does pose a formidable threat to many. The fierce and bitter resistance is a measure of this opposition. Even today, the practice of hypnotism carries with it a risk of criticism or even of loss of status.

It would be desireable for scientifically trained men and women to be open-minded, broad-minded, or just honest enough to examine the evidence before passing judgment or making a comment.

The real advancement of medical science is dependent upon more willingness to check and test the evidence before either rejecting or accepting — even when such evidence threatens to endanger cherished beliefs.

We can anticipate differences having to do with hypnosis to endure. Even among those of us who are using hypnosis

90

the differences are so wide as to appear irreconcilable. If these differences are to be resolved, it can only come from open-minded and honest willingness to test any and *all* claims for hypnosis. Sincere seekers for the truth are required. Nothing can be accomplished by those who seek only to support previously held views. Prejudice has no place in medical or psychological research.

Those of us who use hypnosis regularly have found some areas where we do agree. One area of agreement is that hypnosis is *not* dangerous to the subject. Hypnosis is a state between waking and sleeping—a state we all pass through two or more times each day. Claims by critics that it "might be dangerous" are not supported by facts.

There is agreement that it does not weaken the will nor cause any sort of damage to the nervous system. I know of no evidence showing that hypnosis results in harmful effects to the mind or the body. The hypnotist merely helps the subject prolong the between-sleep-and-waking state long enough to make use of it.

Another point of agreement is that almost anyone can learn hypnotism and can hypnotize almost anyone else. Actually the phrase, "hypnotize anyone else" is incorrect usage. All hypnosis is really self-hypnosis. The person acting as the hypnotist has no more real control over the subject than does a music teacher or instructor of athletes have control over their students.

Whatever the correct phraseology, it is easy to learn the role of hypnotist. Dozens of books on the subject contain instructions for step-by-step induction. No special knowledge or training is required. It is most helpful to have some understanding of human nature and psychology, but not absolutely essential.

My first experience consisted of simply reading an induction technique to a friend from a book—then exchanging roles and having her read the same instructions back to me.

We usally attribute the "power" in hypnosis to the hypnotist. This is not at all correct. Hypnosis is a two-sided relationship. Although the techniques of hypnosis are easily learned, an additional requirement is to have a willing subject. I sincerely doubt that anyone can be hypnotized against their will.

The hypnosis process requires a delicate rapport between the hypnotized and the hypnotist. Some subjects are quick to re spond and are called "good subjects". This merely means that the subject is quickly hypnotized, and easily managed while in the hypnotic state.

There is also the stated belief that some people cannot be hypnotized at all, or only slightly. My experience has shown me that becoming a good subject is learned. Each experience as a subject helps make subsequent responses both more rapid and deeper.

I am frequently asked if anyone can be hypnotized. I believe it is safe to say, "Of course, anyone can be hypnotized." Being hypnotizeable is enhanced by willingness, freedom from fear both of the process and of the one acting as hypnotist, and by repeated exposure to effective induction techniques. The late Dr. Milton Erickson of Phoenix, Arizona, reported a successful hypnosis with a difficult subject after two hundred hours of attempt.

Until and unless the hypnotist can establish a rapport, a willingness of the subject, no state of hypnosis can be induced in any subject. The quality of the rapport between hypnotist and subject determines the quality, or depth of the hypnotic state. This may occur with the first session.

Repeated sessions may be required to prepare someone for childbirth or general anesthesia. Sometimes one hypnotist may be able to succeed where another has failed because a greater rapport has developed.

The determination of whether or not any person can be hypnotized, and the depth to which he can go depends upon his willingness and upon the experience and skill of the hypnotist.

The many misconceptions and misrepresentations have led most people to at first resist hypnosis. Many may be willing to accept the lighter stages. Repeated sessions are usually required to produce the useful greater depths. We all share a natural hesitancy and resistance to the unknown. This resistance can be overcome by a skillful hypnotist who allows the subject enough time to realize the extreme pleasantness of experiencing hypnosis.

Fear of hypnosis can easily be eliminated by simply recognizing hypnosis as a natural phenomenon occurring daily to everyone. If it could be approached with interest and curiosity instead of fear, greater understanding would result. Hypnosis could become widely available and would present an opportunity for all. With the fear and resistance diminished or eliminated, hypnosis becomes the finest of tools for exploring the human mind. Here we have the sharpest of probes with which to dig, to investigate, to examine in careful detail all of the areas and functions of our humanness.

Hypnosis, a natural phenomenon of humans, is as worthy of investigation as any other natural phenomenon. What we have learned so far should be a strong influence in encouraging greater interest and research.

What we do know is most intriguing to those of us who are involved. Our curiosity continues to expand. Some things we do *know*. The phenomenon of hypnosis is real. It is an altered state of consciousness. In this altered state many widely varying changes can be produced. "Lost" memories can be recalled. Physiological changes can be produced. Healing can be accelerated. Self awareness can be elicited. Past lives can be relived. Illnesses of various kinds can be cured, their duration shortened, or their severity decreased.

There are few valid arguments in opposition to the use of hypnosis.

A common misconception is that hypnosis is somehow "dangerous." These allegations are rarely accompanied with any explanation of the kind or extent of the danger that may be present. In my experience there have been few occasions when I considered danger to be present.

It seems to me that the danger is greater for the hypnotist than for the subject. We as hypnotists need to resist the tendency present in so many of us to develop a sense of power out of proportion to the actual power we possess. There is a temptation to use this fantasied power to influence or control family, friends or hypnotic subjects.

Fortunately, subjects appear to have a built-in protection that permits them to refuse any suggestion that would harm them or produce an emotional conflict. Numerous research projects have been attempted to test whether hypnotized subjects could be induced to commit a crime or do a serious anti-social act. No proof that this is a possibility has been produced as of this writing.

One minor danger that can be present, and I have dealt with this in another chapter, is the sudden uncovering of material that is heavily charged with emotion. The hypnotized subject will sometimes, but rarely, begin to show extreme emotion to the point of hysteria. The inexperienced hypnotist could easily become alarmed and want to waken the subject at once. If the subject is wakened before the emotion is fully expended or expressed they will feel uncomfortable. However, if they are allowed and encouraged to express the emotions they are feeling completely before waking, they will feel relieved, relaxed and appreciative when they waken.

My feeling is that even though a few may have suffered distress or minimal harm from the use of hypnosis, far greater harm has been done to people in general by denying them the benefits of hypnosis and therefore prolonging their suffering unnecessarily.

I am convinced that the benefits so far outwiegh the dangers that we are remiss in not using hypnosis to a greater degree. The possible benefits are enormous.

Not only is it possible to produce subjective sensations of changes in touch, taste, smell, hearing, position, temperature, time or identity, but changes that are objectively measurable or observable can also be invoked. Dreams can be recalled, produced and interpreted.

Skin temperature can be raised or lowered. Nausea can be produced or removed. Perspiration can be turned on or off. Bleeding can be increased, slowed or stopped. Blood pressure can be modified. I suspect that every physiological process can be influenced or controlled by hypnotic suggestion. Here is another vast area for research. Can we also influence blood chemistry—and to what extent? Can we remove toxic substances? Can we conquer cancer?

Dr. Carl Simonton reports remarkable benefits from the use of relaxation and visualization in his best-selling book, *Getting Well Again.* Were hypnosis to be used also, the results might be even more successful. Dr. Simonton reports extended life expectancy and even complete remission of cancers that had been diagnosed as terminal, by his methods. If there are techniques that might offer even more, should we not use them?

Inducing hypnosis is so easy and so easily learned—

many people have learned by simply reading a book. No special power is required. Hypnotism is now used by a wide variety of people of all levels of education and experience. Appreciation is growing as to the usefulness and wide benefits to be obtained from hypnosis. There have been surprisingly few documented cases of even minor damage. Whatever dangers that may exist have been greatly exaggerated.

Hypnosis is really all self-hypnosis. The subject is free to accept or reject any suggestion. In my own experience, even patients who were very deep subjects who customarily responded promptly to any request, would suddenly refuse a suggestion which they found to be unacceptable. With the acceptance of helpful suggestions the benefits are almost magic.

My own personal benefit from hypnosis concerns what I had long considered to be a serious handicap. Being of fair complexion and loving the out-of-doors, I often suffered from severe sunburn. On several occasions I was required to stay in bed for days recovering from a sunburn. The pain, the badly swollen skin, the blistering, and the feeling of illness would gradually fade. Since learning to use self-hypnosis this sunburn problem has been completely overcome. Now I am able to stay in the sun as much as I like. When my skin begins to feel hot and turn red, all that is required is for me to sit down in a shady spot, use my self-hypnosis signal, give myself the suggestions that the burning sensation and redness will fade, that my skin will be tanned tomorrow without blistering or discomfort of any kind. I can then continue in the sun without increase of sunburn. It has been effective every time without fail for over twenty years.

Another experience with changing physiology came as a total surprise. In all my thirty-plus years of using hypnosis, nothing has surprised me more.

A good friend, Betty, and I were doing a bit of exploring into what hypnosis could do. We wanted to test how far back in time it was possible to go.

Before we began, she asked, "Can you do anything about this?" Lifting her slacks, revealed legs completely covered with oozing, festering bites. She reported that fleas loved her, even to the point of leaving dogs to feed on her. She could not wear hose in the summer as the secretions would glue them to her legs. She had tried every available insect repellant. None had had the least effect.

I agreed to try to do something — not having the faintest notion of what that something might be. We proceeded with the experiment of going back to primitive times. This proved to be highly entertaining and humerous. We laughed so much our sides ached. When the experiment was over, I began to waken Betty. I used a slow awakening — counting backward from 21 to 1 using alternate figures. I began counting 21,19, 17,15,13, — — at this point I remembered my promise to try to do something about the flea bites. I paused, trying to decide what to do. Here was my subject nearly awakened. She had been trained to go into hypnosis as I counted from 1 to 21, but not from 13 to 21. Then the thought came to me that whatever I did would probably be ineffective anyhow — I didn't know how to stop fleas from biting — so it didn't really matter what I said. I was still giggling from all the humor of the evening and this giggling is obvious on the tape recording.

I said, "Your subconscious mind will do whatever is necessary so that fleas will stop liking the flavor. 11,9,7,5,3,1 wide awake!"

Betty reported that from that evening the fleas did indeed stop liking her. She had no further problems with fleas. This may appear to be a very small thing. I think it is exceedingly important. Here is a situation in which a giggling hypnotist giving facitious suggestions (without expecting any response) to a nearly awake subject, produced a change so profound that a flea could detect the difference.

If this is possible, it is safe to expect that an infinite number of other physical and physiological changes are also possible.

We have come a long way from the superstition and apprehension surrounding hypnosis, its uses and misuses. We have just started on the road to adventurous exploring into the human mind, its power and potential. Hypnosis, I believe, is the best tool for this exploration.

The important discoveries about the human mind have all been linked to hypnosis.

Freud and Breuer, using hypnosis, were able to help patients recall deeply repressed "forgotten" facts and happenings from their childhood. They called the storehouse for this "forgotten" material the *sub*conscious—below the level of conscious awareness. The concept of a subconscious mind has had a tremendous influence on psychological thinking since Freud's time. Few psychologists today doubt the existence of a sub-conscious. Some use the term "unconscious" which has the handicap of being confused with the unconsciousness of coma or general anesthesia. Sub-conscious seems to be the preferable term.

Another chapter in the history of hypnotism's contribution to the understanding of the human mind begins with Phinias Quimby, a European-trained mesmerist who came to America, lecturing and mesmerizing or magnetizing people and healing them of a variety of illnesses and disabilities. One whom he helped was a woman named Mary Baker who had been ill for many years. She became a grateful devotee and student of Quimby.

About this same time a young man named Josiah, whom Quimby had magnetized in a group with others, began to talk spontaneously not about himself, but about the woman in the chair to his right. He announced her diagnosis and recommended treatment. Quimby did as the boy suggested. The woman reported complete recovery.

Quimby then hired Josiah and had him repeat this unusual pattern when hypnotized many times. There were many cures reported. The remedies Josiah recommended were always easily obtained. Quimby grew curious as to whether they were proper medicines for the diagnoses given. To his surprise and horror he learned that few if any of the prescriptions recommended by the sleeping Josiah contained any effective medicinal properties. They were the equivalent of sugar pills—placebos.

He reasoned that the cures had not come from the prescriptions, but instead had come from the expectation of the ailing ones. He dismissed Josiah and changed his lecture pattern, teaching now the powers of the conscious mind—how our thoughts and beliefs can effect our bodies—the power of positive and of negative thought.

Mary Baker — now Mary Baker Eddy — took up this banner and began writing and teaching. She founded the Christian Science Church. From this beginning has come a wide variety of religious and philosophical concepts based on understanding of conscious mind power.

A third chapter in the understanding of the human mind began in 1901 when an unlearned young man, Edgar Cayce, found that when he was hypnotized he possessed abilities far beyond those present in his usual waking state. He was able to diagnose physical illnesses and disorders and recommended treatments which produced many cures. He was seemingly able to tap into the source of all knowledge. He could respond accurately (while hypnotized) to hundreds of different questions on widely varying subjects. When asked the source of this information, he answered that not only was he in touch with the subconscious minds of those who sought his help, but he also had access to a greater source which he called the superconscious. His work spanned nearly 45 years, and has been carefully preserved. The Association for Research and Enlightenment of Virginia Beach, Virginia, has a library filled with material from the Edgar Cayce "readings." This material may be examined by anyone with serious interest. In addition, more than fifty books and booklets have been written about the work of Edgar Cayce.

Edgar Cayce was greatly revered by those who knew him in his lifetime. His fame continues to grow though he died in 1945. Whenever someone would exclaim about his great talent — his great ability to help people — he would gently look them in the eye and say, "You can do it too."

A few others have been able to manifest Cayce-like abilities. No one else has produced work so extensive nor so well documented. Perhaps further development of knowledge about and skill with hypnosis would develop others with similar abilities as Edgar Cayce.

It is difficult for me to understand why it is that a tool as potent as hypnosis has not become a required course for all physicians, paramedics, psychotherapists and educators. It is regrettable that the greatest use of hypnosis is still in the entertainment field.

I do not like to see hypnosis used for a stage performance, but I am appreciative of those magicians and stage hypnotists who kept hypnotism from dying when the medical profession was largely ignoring it. These stage hypnotists have helped preserve for me a tool to use for my own benefit and for the benefit of others.

The persistent taint on the word hypnosis has led many who use it to call it by other names — Progressive Relaxation, Biofeedback, Mind Dynamics, Meditation, Mind Control, Alpha Dynamics and other similar designations. Instructors in these various organizations insist that they are not using hypnosis. We who use hypnosis regularly recognize their training techniques as indistinguishable from training to induce hypnosis.

What remains to be discovered about the human mind requires only interested and trained hypnotechnicians as researchers.

Perhaps the correct way of viewing the process of hypnosis is to think of ourselves as being subject to suggestion at all times. Hypnosis merely moves us along the suggestibility scale toward a greater and greater responsiveness to suggestion, and a closer and closer contact with deeper parts of our own mind, the minds of others and also universal mind.

There are a number of ways to learn to work with hypnosis. Many of the more than 200 books on the subject give specific instructions. Many instructors offer courses either privately or in groups. Some teachers even offer instruction by correspondence. It is impossible to know how many people in the whole country are involved. It seems to me that the time has come for a more orderly and intelligent exploration of all of the uses and possible misuses of hypnosis.

If hypnosis is as dangerous as some people claim, then we should find the dangers and document them fully. If it is as safe as many others claim, then we should publicize this fact and encourage its widespread use.

One problem that seems to hinder some researchers is that the study of hypnosis requires the use of hypnosis. It is not something that can be studied in a vacuum.

The organizations that seem to me to be making the largest contribution to the understanding of hypnosis other than the Association for Research and Enlightenment, Virginia Beach, Virginia; are World Congress of Professional Hypnotists, 9390 Whitneyville Rd. Alto, MI 49302; The Association for Advancement of Ethical Hypnosis, 60 Vose Ave. South Orange, N.J. 07079; and Association for Past-Life Research and Therapy, P. O. Box 20151, Riverside CA. 92516. There may be others also making great contributions that I do not know about.

It is my personal hope that enough people will become adequately trained in the use of hypnosis that hypnotherapy will become available to anyone wishing to have its benefits.

Chapter 9

THE PROBLEM OF ALLERGIES

We shape ourselves the joy or fear
of which the coming life is made
And fill our Future's atmosphere
With sunshine or with shade.

The tissue of the Life to be
We weave with colors all our own,
And in the field of Destiny
We reap as we have sown . . . . .

We live our life again!
Or warmly touched or coldly dim
The Pictures of the Past remain, —
Man's works shall follow him!

John Greenleaf Whittier

Rare is the person who does not at some period of their life suffer from an allergy — a reaction to some substance usually harmless to others.

People who have a special sensitivity to a food or other substance, or to an animal are usually advised to avoid the allergen if they can or are given a long series of desensitization shots. I have not found — even after lengthy search — any reference in the medical literature that mentions an attempt to find the reasons that those persons who manifest allergic reactions react as they do.

I used the same approach to the allergies of my patients that I used for other kinds of illnesses. I would help them into a state of hypnosis and then ask them to tell me why they were reacting in this manner. Answers were usually promptly given, the initial causative event was lived through until the emotion was expended and then the allergy would be relieved.

Following are descriptions of some of the particulary interesting cases of allergy treated in my office.

Marge Tellez had suffered an unusual reaction to cold water for years. She could not be exposed to cold wetness in any way without reacting violently. The inside of her mouth would swell if she drank something cold. If she held an icy drink in her hand, rinsed her vegetables under cold water, handled frozen food packages or rinsed her hands in cool water the skin of her hands would become swollen, cracked and oozing as well as very painful. If she were caught in a rain shower her skin would erupt in great red swollen blotches wherever a rain drop touched her.

She had been to many doctors, the latest before coming to me in Sacramento in 1959 was the University of California Medical School in San Francisco.

There she was presented to staff and student classes as a rare case, her condition was given a name, she was given medication with which she was to inject herself daily and was warned of the danger of showering when alone in the house as cold shower water might prove fatal.

The injections helped a little, but she was still required to avoid cold water as much as possible. She was given no hope of recovery or even remission of her allergy.

When she considered consulting me she was hesitant—even reluctant. She had heard that my patients sometimes talked of former lives. This was totally contrary to the religious doctrines she had been taught. She understood that proper people did not return in new bodies, but waited patiently to be resurrected by the Lord.

Marge reacted uniquely to hypnosis. When I would ask her to go find the cause of her illness, she would spend several minutes describing designs—irregular patterns and colors—even disjointed bits and pieces of scenes she might have gleaned from distorted dreams. Then suddenly, as if the scene had now come into focus, she would describe a wholly believable event.

During the six sessions I spent with Marge, she relived what she said were four different past lives all of which were traumatically linked with cold water. One was of a drowning, one a near drowning. The third was reported gleefully how she (then a galley slave) and the others had overpowered the captain of the ship and had keel-hauled him. Her glee changed abruptly to dismay when she recognized that captain as the man she was now married to.

The most dramatic of the four lives she reported was one during which she and her four children were on their way to colonial America from Europe in a wooden ship. As the ship neared shore, it struck rocks and began to take on water. A powerful swimmer, she was able to swim to shore with two of her children, but was unable to save the other two.

She stood on the shore watching the ship break up knowing it meant the loss of the remaining two children. She expressed all the emotion appropriate to the situation. Only after I helped her relive this exceedingly painful experience several times was she able to talk about it calmly.

After the calm, matter-of-fact relating of the incident, the allergy left and it did not return. A few days later she went trout fishing with her husband in a cold mountain stream without the slightest reaction or discomfort.

I saw Marge regularly for several years following her therapy. It was always one of her delights to go with me for coffee so that she could show me that she could still drink from a glass of ice water — something we all take for granted, but which she had not been able to do before our work together.

Another case was of a severe or excessive reaction to cold temperature. R. S. constantly complained of the cold whenever the weather would cool to 70 degrees or below. Even after adding layers of clothing he would continue to be uncomfortable.

In searching for the cause of this inconvenient, but not disabling pattern, he found and described three past lives in which cold had been associated with his deaths.

In the early days of Texas he had become lost in a blizzard and had frozen to death.

In 1943, he was a Japanese Airforce navigator. He relived vividly an air battle with American planes, during which his plane was hit and his pilot seriously wounded. Though the plane did land, it was on one of Aleution Islands. The pilot died soon from his wounds. The navigator perished more slowly from the cold.

In a much earlier life he had led a Roman legion in battle against Hannibal's forces and elephants. As he recognized the certainty of defeat he had run back through his own men and was shot by a Roman arrow. In this instance too he had suffered from the cold as he was inadequately dressed for the mountain climate.

Each of these past life experiences was relived under hypnosis several times until the emotional expression was calm — almost indifferent. Following this handling of his problem, he became normally tolerant to cold.

One of the most dramatic stories relating to an allergy was from a young woman who could not remain comfortable in the presence of a cat. Her eyes would begin to itch, as would her skin. Then she would begin to have difficulty breathing. If she would remain with a cat for a longer time, she would develop asthma. She liked cats and was unhappy that she could not play with them. This reaction pattern was totally relieved by just one therapy session, the transcript of which follows:

Dr. H.   Please now go back through time and find the reason you are having this trouble with cats.

D. M.   I'm walking

Dr. H.   Where are you walking? Where are you coming from?

D. M.   The camp. Tents.

Dr. H.   What is you appearance? What color is your hair?

D. M.   Black.

Dr. H.   Are you male or female?

D. M.   I'm male.

Dr. H.   What is you name?

D. M.   Orgio.

Dr. H.   How old are you?

D. M.   Twenty eight.

Dr. H.   As you are walking tell us what you are doing

and what you see.

D. M.   I have a spear in my hand and a shield. I'm hunting

Dr. H.   What are you hunting?

D. M.   Intruders. They're fair skinned. North. There are a lot of birds. It's very quiet. I've got to be quiet.

Dr. H.   How many of them are there?

D. M.   Three dozen. I'm running back to tell my chief that there are intruders down by the river. Then right in front of me there is a tiger. I stop in my tracks.

Dr. H.   Is he a big one?

D. M.   About two fifty.

Dr. H.   What happens next?

D. M.   He's lying down looking at me. He's crouched down ready to spring.

Dr. H.   What are you feeling as he looks at you?

D. M.   I'm trying to stay calm and figure out a way to get away.

Dr. H.   How close is he?

D. M.   Ten yards. He's ready to attack if I move. I stand there a long time and then start moving very slowly to my right. I've got my shield up and my spear in my hand. My chest is hurting so much. I'm almost around him. He hasn't turned and looked at me or nothin'. I'm going to try and run. I'm going to have to do it just right.

Dr. H.   Go on. Tell everything that happens.

D. M.   I'm standing behind him. I stand for a little bit longer so he's not too riled when I leave. I'm waiting (Then she began to breath very heavily and rapidly.)

Dr. H.   What's happening?

D. M.   (Expressing great fear) He's comin' after me. (Then a great outcry of anguise and horror together with a flinging of her body violently back in the chair.)

Dr. H.   (Taking her hand) It's all right. You're all right now. Everything is fine. Go back again to the time when you are walking in the forest and everything is quiet and peaceful.

D. M.   (Now speaking calmly) I'm going to tell my chief that there are strangers going to the river. I'm running. I come to a spot and I hear this growling sound and it's a tiger—a huge thing. He's staring at me. I stand and I watch him. He's watching me. I stand there for a long time. He's calmed down now. Somehow I gotta get around him. I can't leave very quickly. I move very slowly around to my right until I'm around behind him. I wait for a while. I'm going to drop my shield and spear and run. (Panting breathing again.)

Dr. H.   What's happening now?

D. M.   I'm scared. He's getting closer—and closer.

Dr. H.   Keep talking.

D. M.   He's breathing on me. I'm not going to make it. I'm not——(Another loud outcry, but not to the extreme of the first one.)

Dr. H.   O.K. Let go. (She quickly became more calm.) Now what's happening? Where are you now?

D. M.   I'm watching.

Dr. H.   What are you watching?

D. M.   I'm watching the tiger eat me.

Dr. H.   How are you feeling about this?

D. M.   It's a shame I had to go that way. I was a very good scout.

106

Dr. H. Where are you watching from?

D. M. The treetops.

Dr. H. Is the fear all gone? (She shakes her head) Let's go through it one more time.

D. M. I'm running and there ten yards in front of me crouched down is a tiger. His hair is raised up and his ears are up and his eyes are right at me. I stop right in my footsteps. I stand there for a long time lookin' at him — a long time.

Dr. H. Are you feeling the fear as you tell it this time?

D. M. A little.

Dr. H. Keep talking.

D. M. I'm just frozen like a statue. I keep moving my thumb on my spear to keep me together. I make my decision to go around him. I start off to the right. It takes a long time to get around him. I'm going to drop my things and run.

Dr. H. Go on. You're running now. Each time you tell it it will be much easier for you.

D. M. (Rather calmly) He's catching up. I can't outrun him. (a heavy grunt, but no outcry)

Dr. H. What happened?

D. M. (Sadly) He tore my back apart.

Dr. H. Are you still feeling the fear? (No response.)

D. M. I'm just sitting there watching him eat me. Face down on the ground. My back is all torn out.

Dr. H. How are you feeling?

D. M. A good warrior should die in battle.

Dr. H. Are you still feeling fear?

D. M. A little bit.

Dr. H. Then let's go over it one more time until the fear is all gone. You're running back to your chief. Tell the whole thing very quickly.

D. M.   I'm running back to my chief to tell him there are strange people that are going down to the river. I hear a sound and I stop cold. There is a tiger right in front of me ... I'm going to make a run for it. I drop everything and I start running.

Dr. H.   If there is any fear left just feel it and let it go. Let go of the fear and go on with your story.

D. M.   I'm running. And he just jumps right up on my back. (This last statement was without emotion. She seemed calm and unconcerned.)

Dr. H.   How is the fear now? Is it all gone? (She nods.) How are you feeling?

D. M.   Upset.

Dr. H.   Let's talk about it until it's all gone.

D. M.   I should have been smarter. I could have gotten away from that animal. I thought so hard.

Dr. H.   Is there anything that you have learned from this experience?

D. M.   To take my time and be more like a cat when I hunt and try to outthink them before they outthink me.

Dr. H.   Do you need to talk about this incident any more? (She shakes her head.) Are there any other times when you have had big trouble with cats? If there is go back and find it.

D. M.   I'm a little girl.

Dr. H.   Tell me all about it.

D. M.   My parents have a barn in the back yard. And there is a whole bunch of cats out there. They told me to never get near them.

Dr. H.   What kind of cats?

D. M.   All kinds! There's a bunch of 'em out there.

Dr. H.   What's your name?

D. M.   Lucy.

Dr. H.   O.K. Lucy, tell me about the cats in the barn. What happened?

D. M.   My daddy won't let me go out there because he says that they're not nice.

Dr. H.   Do you want to go out there?

D. M.   Yeah! I want to play with the kitties. They just had a whole bunch of new kitties. I want to go out and play with them.

Dr. H.   Do you go out there and play with them?

D. M.   Shhhh! Gotta be quiet.

Dr. H.   Do you go out there?

D. M.   (Whispering) Yes, I'm going to go out and look at the kitties. Shhhh. Gotta be quiet.

Dr. H.   O.K. Lucy, tell me what happens.

D. M.   I'm openin' up the door and a whole bunch of kitties are there but no big cats are around. I don't know where the mommies are. I'm goin' in. Shhh. Oh look at em—look at em. Aren't they cute. They're meowing.

Dr. H.   How many are there?

D. M.   Oh there's about seven of em. And in this one there's eight of em. And over here there's four of em. And the one with eight of em they're brown and black. In the one with four of em they're all white. They're so pretty and so little. They don't have their eyes open yet. (Giggling.) I like em. I want to take em home. I wonder if I can stuff em in my pockets.

Dr. H.   Do you?

D. M.   I'm gonna try. I'm gonna try. I'm going to put one in here and one in here. (She made the movements of stuffing the kittens in her pockets and patting them gently.) In my pockets. I'm going to take them home. Now you've gotta be quiet babies — quiet, quiet. I'll get the rest later on. (Humming with pleasure.)

Dr. H.   What do you do with them when you get them home?

D. M.   I'm gonna put em in a box. And put em under my bed. They're so pretty. I gotta make sure they don't say much. I put a towel in there so they'll be warm and let them cuddle up and keep warm. Nobody knows.

Dr. H.   How are you going to feed them?

D. M.   Oh, I gotta eye dropper from my dad's old — — he had sumpin wrong with his eyes. It's a real itty bitty thing, but it'l work. I'm gonna have to draw the milk in it and make sure it doesn't go down their throats too fast. That's how I'm gonna feed em. Gonna feed em tonight after everyone's in bed. That's how I'm gonna do it.

Dr. H.   Does anyone know you have them yet?

D. M.   Nooo. (Chuckling.) I'm the only one. I'm going to go out and get some more tomorrow.

Dr. H.   What are you doing now?

D. M.   It's after dinner and I'm waitin' for Ma and Pa to go to bed so I can feed em. I hear em meowing. I take out the box and I bring it up and I pet them and make sure that they don't meow. They're so nice. They look like little rats. They're so sweet. Well, I gotta feed em. Ma and Pa are in bed now. I'm getting milk for my kitties. Don't eat so fast! You little poopskins. O.K. You've had enough, They're so cute. He really is cute. O.K.You guys go to bed. I'll go get some brothers and sister for you tomorrow.

Dr. H.   O.K. What happens next?

D. M.   I go to bed and go to sleep. I can't stay up all

110

night.

Dr. H.   Do the kitties go to sleep?

D. M.   Yeah, they're asleep. They're all full and fed and warm. They go to sleep.

Dr. H.   What happens next?

D. M.   I'm gettin' up in the morning. I go down and I have breakfast, and fool around. I'm not old enough to help with any of the chores.

Dr. H.   How old are you?

D. M.   Ohhh—five?—four—I'm a itty bitty kid. I'm about five.

Dr. H.   What are you doing now?

D. M.   Thinkin' about gettin' more kitties.

Dr. H.   Is it about time to do that?

D. M.   Yep. It always gets in the afternoon that Mom starts sewin' and doin' stuff inside. Dad's outside feedin' the horses—so I can go to the barn and get more kitties.

Dr. H.   Where are you now?

D. M.   Lookin' out the door makin' sure anyone's not around. Gotta be quiet. (Whispering.) I'm going to sneak out the door. Gotta be quiet. Don't make no noise.

Dr. H.   Does anybody see you?

D. M.   Nope!

Dr. H.   Do you get more kitties?

D. M.   I open up the door, and somethin's not right.

Dr. H.   What's the matter?

D. M.   All the big cats are around—lookin' real wild. I don't like it. I start talkin' to em though—bein' real nice. I go in and I shut the door and I sit down on the step and I talk to em. I tell em that

111

I have a couple o' their kitties. I don't think they understand me very well.

Dr. H.   Lucy, what's going on now?

D. M.   I'm tellin' them that I'm going to take a couple more of their kitties so they'll be safe. I don't think they understand. I get up and I go over to the nest.

Dr. H.   Do you get some more little ones?

D. M.   No! Oww—. No, I can't they won't let me. oww Ooo—They're clawing me all over. Ouch—ooo it hurts. I can't get to the door. They're clawin' me. Ohhh— Why are they doin' that? I'm just tryin' to help them. Owww—oooo.

Dr. H.   How many are there?

D. M.   A whole bunch of em. They won't let me alone. I can't get out the door because they're clawin' me. They're bitin' me.

Dr. H.   Can you holler for Daddy?

D. M.   I, I, I (stammering) He's not around. Mom and Daddy can't hear me. I'm not supposed to be in here. I can't yell. I gotta get out. Ouch! Owe! oww—ooo. I'm trying to get to the door. I'm almost there. I open up the door and I start runnin'. I'm all cut up. I'm bleedin' real bad. My dress is all bloody. I run in to Mommy and I told her that I went in to see the kitties.

Dr. H.   What does Mommy do?

D. M.   She picks me up and holds me. She said, "You know better than that." I said, "I know. I just wanted to see em." And she cleaned me all up and I have scars. There are a couple of big ones on my face.

Dr. H.   Are you feeling better now?

D. M.   I don't feel very good.

Dr. H.   Do you still have the kitties in your bedroom?

D. M.   No, I took em to Mommy. Then she put me to bed. She said I'm gonna have to get a shot or something—or take medicine or something. I don't know. I've got a big long cut down my face. She says that it'll be there for a long time. And the ones on my hands and my legs and my arms.

Dr. H.   Did Mommy put something on them?

D. M.   Yes, she washed em all out and put some ointment that she had on em.

Dr. H.   How do you feel about cats right now?

D. M.   I don't like em. I don't even want to see one again.

Dr. H.   Are you afraid?

D. M.   Yes!

Dr. H.   O.K. Lucy, let's go back over it again. It will be easier this time. We will start out at the place where you are going out the second time to get more kitties. . .

D. M.   (Whispering.) Shhh. You've got to be quiet. I'm going to go out the door and get more kitties. You've gotta be quiet, because mommy and daddy won't let me go out there. Shhhh! I look out the door to make sure no one sees me. Going out. Gonna get more kitties.

Dr. H.   What are you doing now?

D. M.   I'm opening up the door. A bunch of older cats are there now. I walk in, I shut the door and sit down on the doorledge and I talk to them.

Dr. H.   Are they listening to you?

D. M.   Well, they're listening, but the wummies aren't understanding a word I say. I told them I was going to take a couple o' their kitties so that I could help them out, so they won't get cold and die. And I go over to the nest to pick em up and they're scratching me. Ohhh! Ohhh! They're scratching me all over—a whole bunch of em. Some of them get my face.

Dr. H. Are you feeling the fear now?

D. M. No.

Dr. H. All right go ahead and tell me the rest of the story quickly.

D. M. They're just clawin' me. I get to the door and I run to my mommy. I'm sorry.

Dr. H. Go on—Mommy's cleaned you up and put you to bed—

D. M. I'm still bleeding in some places.

Dr. H. Is the fear all gone.

D. M. Mommy will protect me. Yeah. She'll do sumpthin' about it.

Dr. H. Are you sure the cats can't hurt you anymore?

D. M. I just won't go near them any more.

Dr. H. Are you afraid of cats?

D. M. Don't like them. They're not very nice. They're mean.

Dr. H. Is the fear all gone?

D. M. I'm not afraid. I just don't like em.

After just this one session on the cat problem she no longer reacted to cats as previously. She was now able to be around cats—even holding them and petting them without discomfort.

These are three examples of the rapidity with which it is possible to remove the causes of allergies. When the cause is found and the initial emotional charge released through reliving the incident as many times as is necessary for the relief of the emotional tension, the symptoms will disappear and will not return.

Chapter 10

RESPONSIBLE RESPECTABILITY

"Every human being has a work to carry on within, duties to perform abroad, influences to exert, which are peculiarly his, and which no conscience but his own can touch." Wm. Ellery Channing

I am a physician. Since 1949 I have been licensed in the State of California to "Use any and all methods of treating the sick."

When I found that the methods of treating I had been taught in Medical School fell far short of the ideal, I began to examine other possibilities — to look beyond what I had been taught. The lack I sought to fill concerned the relationship of our thoughts and our emotions to our body functions.

I felt exceedingly ignorant and untrained in this area. I was dissatisfied with training that had left so large a gap in my understanding. Not until I began using hypnosis regularly did I feel I was really meeting the needs of those who came to me. Although it is legal for me to practice psychotherapy and to use hypnosis in such practice, I did not learn hypnosis in medical school. My training in hypnosis came to a far greater degree from people outside the medical profession than from within it.

My interest in the human mind, the human spirit, the human soul had begun when I was very young. I was curious about everything and wanted to know not just what and how, but *why* things happened. I was about ten years old when a wave of interest in the power of "mind over matter" became known to me. Knoxville, Iowa, where I lived then, was full of discussions of this subject. I was fascinated by the idea of "mind over matter". It was exciting to listen to adults talk about this new idea.

115

I was particularly impressed by reports of a test conducted by a group of young men in town.

The group decided to find out if suggestion could make a well person ill. A local merchant, who frequently boasted that he had never been sick a day in his life was selected as their target. Each day one or more of these young men would stop by his store and drop a carefully planned remark such as, "Are you feeling all right? You don't look yourself, Mr. Miller." Or they might say, "You look a little pale." or, "Gee, you've gotten thin — Are you ill? I've never seen you look that way." or "Aren't things going right, Mr. Miller? You look so worried."

Within two weeks Mr. Miller (not his real name) was in the hospital seemingly seriously ill. The group became frightened at what they had done. They went to the hospital together and confessed. Mr. Miller promptly improved and returned to his former state of good health. I am sure that my knowledge of this incident has influenced my thinking greatly.

A little later I read a book by Sir James Jeans, *The Mysterious Universe*, having to do with space, time and material. Time was spoken of as being another dimension, and explanation given of concepts beyond those easily observed in the world. This opened up areas of thinking and questioning not previously examined by me. My curiosity was further stimulated. I wanted to read and to test whatever I read. I read voraciously. I tested wherever I could.

A book, *Palmistry For All*, by Cheiro, began a new chapter of exploration. I found that some of the things in the book were applicable to myself, friends and family. The size, shape, color, texture, as well as the lines of hands do denote characteristics appropriate to the owners of the hands.

I could amuse or entertain with my knowledge of hands and was even able to earn money reading palms for parties, fund raising events and in a tea room. It was not necessary to resort to faking, as it is possible to tell a great deal about a person by merely examining the hands.

Because of my interest and growing reputation, I was privileged to meet and get to know a number of most interesting people whose lives were in some way involved with mental, psychic or soul phenomena. From each I gathered new information which I would test in my own experience as best I could.

My interests excluded nothing from the whole spectrum of the mental and psychic. I would observe or read about almost everything. I wanted to find out all I could. It didn't take long to realize that there were widely differing views on every subject. Therefore I would reserve judgment on the validity of each idea until I could test it myself. I found myself at an early age establishing a pattern that has been most useful. I neither accept nor reject an idea or concept on the basis of authority or reports of someone elses observation. When I can test myself, and *only* when I can test, do I feel comfortable with an idea.

I was disappointed in medical school with the lack of attention to the inner spirit of man. We were provided good instruction about the structure of the human body and its function as related to structure. Also included was a great deal of instruction about the human brain. I felt a sense of lack that more could not be taught—mainly because so little is really known. One brief course in psychiatry left me intrigued but dissatisfied. Some of us formed a neuropsychiatric club to which we could invite outside speakers in an attempt to fill the void in our education. My first exposure to hypnosis was at one of our meetings. We had invited a hypnotist to speak and to present a demonstration. Again the doors of my curiosity widened. I wanted to know more.

This search led into many areas. One particularly exciting adventure included the phenomenon of inspired writing in which an unseen entity, Patience Worth, "sent through" poetry of incredible beauty and statements of deep insight. This material was produced through a friend of mine, much of it in my presence. In 1971 I self-published a collection of this writing in a book I called *I Knew Patience Worth.*

I showed some of the Patience Worth material to the late Don Blanding, well known poet, and asked his opinion of it.

Don Blanding not only said that the material was good poetry, but that much of his own poetry came to him in the same manner. He suggested that I read *There is a River*, a biography of Edgar Cayce, by Thomas Sugrue, and a series of books by Stewart Edward White, including *The Betty Book, The Unobstructed Universe, Across the Unknown* and *The*

Job of Living.

The story of Edgar Cayce is most impressive for its extensive documentation as well as the nature of the psychic phenomena. Edgar Cayce, a man totally unschooled could do remarkable things. He could put himself into a deep hypnotic state, during which he could answer questions put to him on many subjects. Most of his work had to do with diagnosing the ailments of both strangers and people known to him and recommending treatments for their illnesses. These people could be in the same room with Cayce or at a distance — perhaps even thousands of miles away. He used medical terms when hypnotized that were far beyond his conscious understanding. Some remedies he recommended were so old as to be almost lost. Others were so new that they were not yet in wide use.

Edgar Cayce did this work for nearly forty-five years, the last twenty of which were in Virginia Beach, Virginia. He was investigated by a number of scientifically trained persons. Some came to appreciate and admire Cayce. Others left shaking their heads in puzzlement and wonder. None were able to find the evidence of fraud that they expected.

As I first read of Edgar Cayce in 1949, I neither accepted nor blindly rejected the story. I kept the material in abeyance until I could check it out myself. If I could demonstrate a fact unmistakeably, then it would be unimportant whether anyone else had produced similar material fraudulently or honestly. I wondered if the Cayce material could prove to be helpful to my patients.

I learned all I could about hypnosis. I submitted to the hypnotic procedures of others. Slowly I began to use hypnosis in my medical practice. I was then in family general practice, which afforded many opportunities to use hypnosis. I started very cautiously. I used hypnosis for anesthesia to ease the pain of painful shots, to ease a headache, to do minor surgery, to get people to relax during a manipulative treatment and for other minor psychosomatic complaints. I then tested it in the management of pregnancy and childbirth.

My interest in hypnosis grew until it took precedence over interest in other modalities. I gradually eliminated all cases except those who were ill because of psychosomatic problems. I began to use hypnosis with nearly every patient who came to me. I did this at a time when public acceptance was just beginning to develop.

Then a change in the public attitude toward hypnosis occurred. This change was hastened by the appearance of what was spoken of as a publishing freak. The book, *The Search For Bridey Murphey*, by Morey Bernstein, flashed across the country in 1956, becoming an instant best seller. It related how a Peublo, Colorado, housewife under hypnosis reported a previous life as Bridey Murphey in Ireland in 1806. The success of this book sparked a great interest both in hypnosis and in reincarnation.

Both the book and its author were severely castigated with criticism. My own reaction was one of being pleased that this non-medical book written by a non-medical person turned the tide of interest to hypnosis after it had been almost totally ignored for two hundred years.

It is my belief that the interest generated by the Bridey Murphey book was probably a very great influence leading to the official recognition in 1958 by the American Medical Association of hypnosis as an acceptable medical therapy.

As a result of this belated approval, doctors no longer need fear loss of their professional status if they use hypnosis in their practice.

We users still face the scorn of some of our colleagues. We are sometimes looked upon as though we are just barely members of the fraternity.

Among those who use hypnosis as a therapy there are two main groups. Most use the directive or commanding techniques. A few use non-directive, its opposite. The use of one or the other is usually a matter of preference. It also depends on what the hypnotist understands about human nature. The directive method—used primarily for symptom removal or behavior modification—assumes that the hypnotist knows how to remedy any problem of the subject, and does so by direct suggestion. This can become a misuse of the hypnotic techniques if symptoms are simply removed without also dealing with the cause or causes of the symptoms.

The method of choice, I believe, is non-directive or permissive. This method has the advantage of creating a situation of self-help in which the subject has the chance to find his or her own answers and prescribe the proper remedies, rather than having this all done by the hypnotist.

In this method the subject is helped to go into a deep hypnotic state (and it is all self-hypnosis) and then is asked to seek within the memory record to find the cause or causes of the complaints. The subject is also asked to give recommendations for changes or corrections.

Hypnosis is the tool. The hypnotist is the helper. The subject is the source of all necessary information to deal with any problem. With this tool we successfully uncover and reveal memories and emotions that may have lain buried deep inside the subject for a very long time.

Whatever the complaint, the method is the same — directing the hypnotized subject to seek and find the answers to any problem. This method is so successful that it seems correct to assume that each human psyche contains all the information needed to recognize, understand and correct any human ill. The task is simply to probe into the subconscious mind and uncover the cause, call it into the consciousness and dissipate the buried emotions that may be attached to it. If the subject is filled with fear, as was B. E. then he or she is led to look for its cause, and is provided support and guidance as required in the search.

This therapeutic attitude is compatible with the psychoanalytic method. It differs in that in the psychoanalytic situation the patient must struggle to bring forth the repressed material slowly and with great effort without the aid of the hypnotic trance state. I have long suspected that in successful psychoanalysis, deeply repressed material is recalled only when the patient spontaneously enters the hypnotic state.

Whether or not I am correct about psychoanalysis, I am certain that therapeutic progress with the aid of hypnosis is many times more rapid than is therapy without hypnosis. The differance between psychotherapy using hypnosis and therapy using the usual psychoanalytic, is that in the first hidden memories are revealed much more quickly and probably more deeply than in the second.

My use of the term subconscious may contain meanings which differ from those used by most psychotherapists. I include all that area of mind which is below, or beyond the level of conscious mindness. This area is often referred to as the soul. By whatever designation, it seems to me that here all our memories are stored, here all our troubles originate and here all solutions can be found and all problems resolved. Perhaps my use of the term is rather more inclusive than different from that used by others.

There are those therapists who resist the inclusion of religious discussion into therapy. I found it imperative to deal with religious teachings, thoughts and feelings. Most of my patients' problems included serious conflicts in the catagory of religion — guilt, confusion regarding right and wrong, fear of punishment in the after-life, of Hell-fire, of isolation, of alienation, of the wrath of God and of lack of inner security and peace that can come from a real understanding of our universe and of our relationship to the universe, to universal forces or to God. Much of the fear I encountered in my patients was related to the overzealous or deliberately intentional use of fear by ministers and priests seeking to impress parishioners with the need for conforming behavior.

The resultant was the production of all sorts of repressions of feelings into the subconscious, thus producing a condition of clogging or binding up of these feelings, these traumatic memories. When strong feelings are long suppressed this prevents any real communication with our inner selves. Whatever school of psychology is followed, the primary problem is to reestablish the lost contact with inner thoughts and wisdom.

The subconscious mind, when probed, explored, drained of buried painful records, restored to balance, becomes a source of strength and insights to meet all situations. This probing requires that we dig into the areas of repressed feelings and thoughts, that we purge the emotional charge from these areas. The memories remain when this is done. Only the pain is gone.

It all seems so simple!

Using hypnosis makes it possible to attain clarification of confusion, examine basic human nature, define the applicability of theological concepts and teachings. We can test any concept to determine its validity, its containment of truth or falsehood.

The material produced by my subjects over a span of more than thirty years has always been compatible with itself. Even though the background of these subjects were widely varied, and their approaches to life when not hypnotized often incompatible, when they were hypnotized these wide variations disappeared. They agreed with one another—and with the material produced by the sleeping Edgar Cayce—particularly was there high agreement in their experiencing past lives and reporting the consequences of past deeds, thoughts and vows.

The material is also compatible with the highest concepts of all major religions. Sacred scripture of all religions including the Judeo-Christian, contain numerous passages referring to and supporting reincarnation and karma, the nature of death and afterlife, of between lives, the process of choosing to be reborn and the factors entering into the choice of parents.

When I speak before groups of students, the idea of choosing parents always draws a big reaction from my audience. It seems important to me to further check this possibility. If this is valid—if we do indeed choose our parents—then the proper understanding of this fact would be an excellent basis for improving parent-child relationships.

This understanding has been a great personal help to me. With my first two sons, I could obtain almost immediate moderation of their teen-age rebellious attitudes and actions by threatening to return as their child. With my third son, all that was required was just to ask him to think about how he would feel about a son of his own with attitudes and actions identical to his own, and emphasizing that that is the way that karma works. After a period of quiet thought he would make an abrupt change to be more pleasant and cooperative.

Perhaps this use of hypnosis can become a powerful aid to parents and their children, both of whom suffer from the lack of such information.

Hypnosis can also be a great aid in bringing about an understanding of the true nature of the major events of our lives.

Everyone has a deep-seated drive to discover the secrets behind the mystery of the cycle of life. Lacking complete answers, we stumble about in confused searching. We stand in awe of the mystery of birth. We confront death without comprehending its true nature. We see only a tiny segment of our total experience with our conscious minds alone. At deeper levels, reachable by the use of hypnosis, these seemingly unanswerable riddles become less and less obscure and life becomes both more meaningful and more manageable.

The riddles of life are so intimate, so basic, so meaningful that man cannot exist comfortably without having answers to them. Fortunately an answer is available.

Although I am not here making claims of proof of my findings—proof of reincarnation—I would however like to provide a few comments and quotes that may give courage to the hesitant so that they can explore an area so threatening to the medical, psychological and ecclesiastical establishments.

Among the well known histroical great thinkers who espoused and taught the doctrine of reincarnation and karma are Pythagoras, who wrote of his own former life memories; Pindar the poet; Anaxagoras, the philosopher; Plato and his student, Aristotle; also Plutarch and Plotinus.

Ovid, the great, of Rome said, "And as the pliable wax is moulded into new forms, and no longer abides as it was before, nor preserves the same shape, but yet is the same wax, so I tell you the soul is ever the same, but passes into different forms."

During the heighth of the Roman Empire, philosophers, writers, leaders of political and religious groups spoke of reincarnation as though there was no doubt about the industructibility or the immortality of the human soul. These included Julius Caesar, Cicero, Virgil, and the Emperor Julian.

Two of the three major sects within Judiasm accepted reincarnation. Only the Sadduccees taught that the soul died with the body. Both Essenes and the Pharasees taught that the soul survives and returns again in a new body.

As I reread my Bible, I find so many references to support and illustrate our immortality and our need to return to Earth again and again until we have perfected ourselves enough to rejoin and remain with our Creator.

My Bible, particularly the New Testament has uncounted illustrations and supportive statements regarding reincarnation and karma. My personal favorite is from Galations, Chapter 6, Verse 7. "Whatsoever a man soweth, that shall he also reap."

My patients find during their search within that they are indeed reaping what they have sown. The sowing included thoughts, vows, wishes as well as acts.

When a troubled or ill person is able to see that they have contributed to their own problems by their own past choices, they see the necessity of making new and different choices. They see the need to sow better seeds for future reaping. When these people stop blaming parents, society, economic conditions or other influences for their problems and begin to assume full responsibility for themselves, a big step toward maturity is taken.

A real understanding of how the principles of reincarnation and karma work for everyone gives a special kind of freedom. No longer is it necessary to view ourselves as helpless victims in an uncaring world. We can now take charge of our life situations, prepare ourselves for future reaping of the good rewards from the sowing of good seeds now.

Chapter 11

IS IT THEN?

Let us return to reincarnation ... for there never was a more beautiful, a juster, a more moral, fruitful and consoling, nor to a certain point, a more probable creed ... It alone, with its doctrine of successive expiations and purifications, accounts for all the physical and intellectual inequalities, all the social inequities, all the hideous injustices of fate.

Maurice Maeterlinck,
— — Our Eternity

I am not asserting that we have "scientific" proof of reincarnation. I do claim that we who choose to believe it find ourselves not only on very solid ground, but in excellent company.

The weight of argument does not rest, however, on either the time span a belief has been held, nor on the number of great minds who have held the view. The greater weight of evidence lies in the fact that apparently everyone can report memories of other lives. Nearly everyone can report numerous incidents in which they suddenly "knew" someone or some place not previously seen in this present life.

Additional evidence is the existence of exceptional talent. A child who manifests unusual musical abilities for composition or performance at a very young age may be drawing on things learned before.

Other outstanding talents are also probable carryovers from previously learned skills. All other attempts to explain such unusual and unlearned mastery prove less satisfactory than does the reincarnation and karma concept.

The sudden strong emotional response to a person at a first meeting—either feelings of attraction or of fear or revulsion is easily understood when we accept the probability that we have known that person before.

If the doctrines of reincarnation and karma are so easily demonstrated, if they answer questions unanswerable by other reasoning, if they present a view of life that leads to responsible self-evaluation and mature choices, if they enable the ill and suffering — the fearful and troubled — to find relief, then why are they not universally taught and accepted?

To understand this *why* we need to review some of the history of thought concerning the reincarnation concept. Through the history of opposition to the ideas of reincarnation and karma runs a heavy thread illustrating how opponents fought these ideas because they appeared to interfere with their drive to obtain and sustain power.

All religions, at least in their early development contained or included a belief in reincarnation and karma. As these new religions gained converts, powerful persons or groups assumed control of them and changed the teachings in ways to protect their power position.

Early Christian writers such as Justin Martyr, St. Clement, St. Gregory, St. Jerome, St. Augustine, Synesius, Lactonius and Origen taught and wrote of the truth of reincarnation.

A.D. 325 can be said to be the birth year for the Bible as a *book*. In that year Constantine the Great called a council of bishops to meet in Nicea to determine which among the many early writings were worthy of inclusion as truly divinely inspired and which were of questionable origin. The bishops were of varying beliefs. The task must have been most difficult and the atmosphere charged with dissension, jealousy, intolerance and bigotry. It seems most probable that some of the choices both for inclusion and exclusion were less than divinely inspired themselves.

Constantine planned to make the then little-known Christian sect a state religion of the Rome Empire. He made it known that there must be a settling of devisive differences and an agreement of what the Christians really believed.

Papus, historian for the council told of the differing views that prevented agreement. To resolve these differences, it was decided to place all of the books that were to be judged under the communion table and to ask the Lord to make the selection by lifting the books of His choice up on to the top of the table during the night. Papus reports that, "It happened accordingly." The rejected texts were left under the table. Many modern thinkers find it easier to think that the "miracle" was likely promulgated by some of the more enterprising bishops.

Though some of Constantine's biographers depict him as being a devout Christian, it appears more likely that he made use of this new order to gain power. He made it a crime punishable by death for anyone to fail to conform to the then-accepted dogma of the Christian Church.

This pattern of Constantine's marked the beginning of centuries of cruelty and murder in the name of a God of peace and love.

Even though the Council of Nicea eliminated most of the early writings concerning reincarnation from the list of accepted "inspired" books, there still remained a strong influence for belief in reincarnation and karma well into the sixth century, for it was in 533 A.D. that a second council was called—this time in Constantinople.

This council was also called by an emperor, Justinian I, of the Byzantine Empire. He was a man of exceptional abilities which he used to reframe the civil code and build a powerful empire. Then he started to take control of the Church. His control of the church authorities at Constantinople was complete. When he examined the teachings of the various church leaders, he found much that he disliked, declared these teacher heretics, and demanded that they be removed.

Pope Vigilius tried to make peace by insisting that there be equal representation by eastern and western bishops on the council. Justinian ignored this recommendation in his call. As a result, only six of the 165 bishops present were from the west.

Pope Vigilius was in Constantinople at the time but refused to attend the sessions. This casts serious doubt as to whether this council was an official body, and whether its decisions are binding on anybody today.

The council did accede to Justinian's demands and pronounced fifteen anathemas—official church curses. One of these states: "Whoever shall support the mythical doctrine of the pre-existence of the soul and the subsequent *wonderful* opinion of its return, let him be anathema."

I am amused at the wording of this statement. Calling it a *wonderful* opinion suggests that the statement was written by someone who was at least in sympathy if not in full agreement with the concept of reincarnation and karma.

Now, centuries later, we are still being influenced by the acts of two power-glutton emperors. Now we still do homage to the dictates of ancient rulers, thus depriving ourselves of the very hope that inspires man to do his best, to deal justly with his fellow man, to find beauty, consolation, justice and harmony in the universe and in the great design of God. How foolish are those who reject this concept for the traditional church view of everlasting punishment or reward based on a few rigid professed beliefs.

Many religionists, particularly those members of the conservative wing of the Protestant tradition called Fundamentalists still protest loudly in opposition to the reincarnation concept. They are able to seemingly refute this idea through the use of highly selective Bible references.

I, a confirmed and convinced reincarnationist, find abundant supporting references in the Bible. I do no intend to list them all, but will share a few choice passages.

In the *Book of Proverbs*, chapter eight, King Solomon tells it this way, "I was set up from everlasting, from the beginning, or ever the Earth was. When there were no depths, I was brought forth . . . . Before the mountains were settled, before the hills was I brought forth . . . when he appointed the foundations of the Earth. Then I was by him, as one brought up with him; and I was daily his delight, rejoicing always before him; rejoicing in the habitable part of his Earth; and my delights were with the sons of men."

Matthew, in the eleventh chapter, verses 13 and 14, quotes Jesus as saying John the Baptist, "For all the prophets and the law prophesied until John. And if ye will receive it, this is Elias, which was for to come."

In the seventeenth chapter, Matthew repeats this theme in a slightly different way. Verse ten contains a question from Jesus' disciples, "Why then say the scribes that Elias must come first?"

Jesus answered, "Elias truly shall come, and restore all things. But I say to you, that Elias is come already, and they knew him not, but have done unto him whatever they listed . . . ." Then the disciples understood that he spoke unto them of John the Baptist.

The Gospel of John, chapter nine opens with the story of Jesus and his disciples passing by a man who was blind from birth.

His disciples asked Jesus who had sinned, this man or his parents that he had been born blind. Jesus answered that in this case neither—but that the works of God be made manifest in him.

This conversation between the disciples and Jesus clearly indicates that the ideas of reincarnation and karma were a part of their thinking. Without an understanding of the carryover from past lives such a question as "Did this man sin that he was born blind?" becomes absurd. Such a question is consistent only with the understanding of karmic law of reward and punishment from patterns of a previous life. Such operation of karma determines our state of being and conditions of the present life.

St. John in Revelations, 3:12, states the whole concept of the law of reincarnation and karma in just one sentence. "Him that overcometh will I make a pillar in the Temple of God, and he shall go out no more."

This passage certainly supports the idea that Earth life is a training and testing ground for growth and strength-gathering to overcome our animal urges and selfish desires so that we may complete the course, graduate and not be required to again return to Earth.

Several years ago I taught a class in the Extension Division of Sacramento State University entitled, *Psychology, Religion and Reincarnation.* On the final examination one student wrote, "I don't believe reincarnation yet, but I find myself living as though I did." This is far more important than whether it is *believed* or not—that we live as though we expect to truly reap what we are sowing.

Vicarious atonement falls far short of having this effect on the thoughts and actions of those who so believe.

Here is evidence, if not proof, of reincarnation and karma. Is there evidence refuting these ideas? The strongest case against reincarnation is that nonbelievers choose not to accept any of the evidence.

Nothing will sway the person who is determined not to be swayed. I would like to present a challenge to the non-believers that they repeat what I have done and gather their own evidence. I have looked. I have found evidence which satisfies my requirement of proof. This new expanded understanding serves to strengthen and enrich my life. I am comfortable and satisfied. Others must find their own proof or disproof.

I recall a quote from *The Laws of Psychic Phenomenon*, by Hudson. He was discussing investigators of spirit phenomena and said, "Unfortunately, all who investigated became believers and therefore unreliable witnesses." We who have investigated the human mind using hypnosis and have become believers in what we have found are also labeled unreliable — perhaps this is a burden any pioneer in the realm must carry.

Chapter 12

GOING BACK IN TIME

"As long as you are not aware of the continual law of Die and Be Again you are merely a vague guest on a dark Earth."   Johann Wolfgang Von Goethe

There are hundreds of techniques to induce the hypnotic state. Each hypnotist chooses his favorite or favorites. It does not matter whether one or another method is used if the results are attained. More important than choice of method is an understanding of the process and comprehension that there are deep unexplored areas in every human consciousness.

I prefer a slow, permissive technique. When I am working with one person, I like to take their hand in mine — usually left hand to left hand — and in a low monotonous voice talk them into deep relaxation. I always intersperse reassuring phrases and reminders that they are in control and will remain in control — — that they are free to reject anything or everything I say that becomes displeasing, disturbing or conflict-producing. I add that their deep inner wisdom will reject any suggestion that would be detrimental or damaging, and will ignore any request for information that is best not known by the subject at the time.

Holding the hand has several advantages. It gives the subject — especially if it is the first experience with hypnosis — a greater sense of security. It also gives me a more accurate measure of the degree of relaxation. I can feel the hand and arm grow limp and heavy. This tells me how rapidly or how slowly the subject is responding. Some will relax very rapidly. Others require several training sessions before they allow themselves to relax and respond.

When I am working with more than one person at a time,

I modify this from necessity. However, lacking hand contact during the induction, I am less able to determine the speed of response. I therefore proceed even more slowly when with a group.

My favorite induction method is to ask the subject to close the eyes and get as comfortable as possible, with hands unclasped and legs uncrossed. I then direct them to give very close attention to their body beginning with the toes and moving the attention slowly up and over the entire body, arms and head. When they have had time to do this I request that they now give special attention to their breathing, feeling the air pass into the nostrils, up through the upper nasal passages, down through the large and small airways all the way to the bottom of their lungs — then to notice how this process is reversed as they exhale. I suggest that they now imagine that what they are breathing in is pure relaxation, and that what they are exhaling is all the tensions, worries, irritations, fears and pressures from all sources. I tell them to allow the relaxation that has filled their lungs to be carried all over the body, and that the tensions anywhere in the body will be allowed to flow up to the lungs and out with the exhaled breath.

I keep up a steady patter while they are doing this telling them that they are relaxing, getting loose, limp, comfortable, calm, serene, and deeply relaxed. I watch for tell-tale signs of deep relaxation such as increased pallor of the skin, slowing of the breathing or lack of movement of any part of the body.

When the subject appears to be deeply relaxed, (I prefer using the term *relaxed* rather than *sleep*.) I will usually give a few tests of depth.

I first lift an arm and drop it. If it falls limply like a wet rag, then I know they are well relaxed. I will probably then touch their eyelids lightly stating that the lids are locked tightly closed. I they are unable to open the lids, I may go on to other tests in the following order. First the rigid arm that cannot be bent, then the glove anesthesia. If I am training someone to be used in a demonstration before an audience, I proceed on to positive and negative hallucinations. I often also suggest that they have an amnesia for a number, a word or their own name. These tests serve the purpose both of letting me know where the subject is on the depth scale, and also letting the subject know that he or she is really in a hypnotic state. Whatever test is given must always be removed before awakening or at a given signal after the subject is awake. If this is not done they are likely to waken in discomfort or feel uncomfortable for several hours after the hypnotic session is over.

When the subject has reached a sufficient depth for work, it becomes relatively easy. The most difficult part is the induction. Then all there is to do is the gentle leading, or travelling with them through the memory records to find and reveal the sources of their problems.

Each response becomes the basis for the next question. I, like a meticulous archeologist, carefully dig for more information or more clarification.

No matter how lacking in awareness a person may be in his usual waking consciousness, he is able to tap into great wisdom at deeper levels when in hypnosis.

Whatever the complaint, I will suggest, "Now go back to the beginning of this problem. Go back as far as necessary to find the origin and the cause of what is troubling you now."

The response may be almost instantaneous or may require additional time and guidance. If there seems to be an inability to find the requested information it may be helpful to suggest that the subject is in a theater watching something on the screen where images are appearing, or he may prefer to walk down a path in his imagination relating whatever he notices along the path. Another useful fantasy is to guide the subject down a long hallway with many doors on either side, asking him to choose a door and go through, telling what is found on the other side. This is quite preferable to directive or commanding hypnotic procedures. This method does not require the assumption of an omnipotent and omniscient position and does not necessitate directing the subject to do whatever the hypnotist decides is best. Symptoms can be removed by the directive methods. Causes of symptoms cannot be dealt with. When causes are not removed, then symptoms usually recur.

Users of the directive method assume that the pain or other symptom is the problem, and direct removal is the purpose of the treatment. In the non-directive method the pain is thought of as a signal of something deeper. Finding and dealing with the cause is the purpose of treatment. The directive method requires more extensive training and educating of the hypnotist. He then removes the pain through his use of this superior training and knowledge.

The non-directive hypnotist is more a technician who helps the subject discover, understand and remove his symptom through the subjects deeper wisdom, knowledge and power.

Once a contributing event has been found and re-lived, I ask if the emotions expressed are still there. If any painful feeling remains, the subject is requested to go back over the entire happening again, adding any details they may have left out with the first telling. Each time the incident is relived and retold the emotional intensity is diminished until finally the story can be related with complete composure. All that remains is a memory. The painful emotion is neutralized. The cause is removed. The symptom or the illness is permanently relieved.

One of the more dramatic cases that illustrates the need to relieve the stored emotional pressures was the case of Kitty Brown (not her real name.)

Kitty came to me asking me to help her resolve a troublesome conflict. Among her acquaintances was a man for whom she felt intense attraction alternating with equally intense revulsion. Kitty was married to a dependant and somewhat immature man, but she felt content in the marriage and was not seeking out another man. Neither her attraction nor her revulsion to the acquaintance made sense to her. She could find no explanation for either feeling, which were becoming so troublesome that she felt she must have some help to resolve the ambivalence.

The first three sessions with Kitty were unproductive of any relevant material. During the fourth session she related feeling herself standing on a hilltop overlooking a valley. She could describe the valley, and feel the gentle breeze blowing back her long light brown hair. She also felt deep sorrow. No other details were given.

The following session found Kitty again on the hilltop. She said that she went to the hill because she wanted to think. In the valley was a small village. Session by session she would add details. She lived in one of the houses in the village. She had an illegitimate son, still a baby. Bit by bit over a number of sessions, she revealed that she lived alone with her child, a social outcast shunned by the other villagers. The first real breakthrough came during a session during which she relived a day in which she had gone up on the hill to commune with her inner self leaving her infant son asleep in his crib as she had done countless times before. When she returned this day she found that the baby had wakened, had left his crib, had crawled across the floor and had fallen face down in the hot coals of the fireplace. She felt terribly guilty about this. This added more weight to the guilt she felt for bearing him out of wedlock.

She said she know there was something more about the house she needed to know. She felt that if she could move to the house and look into the window, she would know what it was.

Several sessions later she was able to approach the house and to reluctantly look into the window. Then she started to scream. She screamed and moaned for several minutes. I calmed her as best I could be saying, "It's all right. You can scream about this, but you do not need to be afraid of it. Whatever it is, it is now in the past. Just relax and tell me what you see."

The tension slowly left her. She told me what she had seen in the window. She said, "I see my body hanging by a rope from the rafters. I see my baby crawling across the floor and reaching up toward the body. I see my *real* self over in the corner observing the scene and helpless to do anything about it.

Further sessions filled in further details until the whole story was revealed. Her lover in that life was the man who now both attracted and repelled her. She had loved and hated him then. The feeling stored deep within her memory kept surfacing again and again. The old love was mixed with her distress and agony of being deserted when pregnant and left to fend for herself in a bigoted, narrow and unforgiving village. The added guilt of seeing her child's scarred burned face left her with no solution she thought except to hang herself. Then when her real self saw what she had done — that she had not really died, but had really merely deserted her helpless child, the guilt became even more overpowering.

As a result of our work together, Kitty was able to deal with the love-hate ambivalence and to understand the clinging dependency of her husband whom she recognized as the child she had deserted in that life. This was one of the most difficult problems brought to me. Kitty had reason to resist knowing her past history.

Although I do not attempt to direct a subject to a specific traumatic event, it is necessary to help them stay with the event until it is resolved. Patients are reluctant to relive old painful times. However, force is never used—rather a persistent repetitious pursuasion. My patients have shown even greater resistance when I have tried to move them to or through a scene too rapidly.

To move from one scene to another, or from one time period to another, is very simple. I suggest that they go forward or backward in time to an important happening. Sometimes I count from one to five saying that at the count of five they will be at the scene.

Sometines I ask that they give me a signal when they have completed the move. This can be a nod of the head or the lifting of a finger. When the signal is given, or if I notice changes of expression that denote emotion, I will ask a question. "What's happening?" is one of my favorite questions as it is totally non-leading of the subject and allows complete freedom to say whatever they wish to say.

The time required to find significant information varies widely. Some respond with surprising rapidity. Others may have to be led slowly and patiently to recognize and to describe scenes charged with great emotional pain. The reluctant ones are often helped by imagry techniques. It may be necessary to try two or three such techniques. Whichever method that works is the one to use.

Some subjects in their usual waking consciousness object to the idea of going back into other lives. I therefore avoid suggesting that they go back to a particular point. I ask only that they go to a time of significance for helping in the understanding of themselves. Hypnosis has been so grossly distorted in fiction, drama and film that it often takes special effort to convince the subjects that memory recall either recent or distant is possible.

Justin Arnold (not his real name) was one who needed to be shown. He suffered from recurrent stomach ulcers and often felt extremely lonely and depressed. He was a very intelligent professional person in his early thirties. Justin doubted everything. He questioned my qualifications as a doctor because I was a woman. He doubted the value of hypnotism. He did not think he could be hypnotized. He especially doubted that there was anything about age regression that could help him. He even considered age regression as impossible.

If anything these doubts helped, for he quickly became a very good hypnotic subject. Expecting nothing, his resistance was minimal. Early in the second session Justin began to tell about Christmas when he was six years old. He was standing at the blackboard in his school room with his favorite girl friend. Here is the transcript.

Dr. H.   What's your girl friend's name.

J. A.   Jean.

Dr. H.   What's your name?

J. A.   Justin.

Dr. H.   I am going to count back one more year and you will be five. 1,2,3,4,5. Now you are five years old. Find a happy time and tell me about it.

J. A.   I'm with my grandma.

Dr. H.   Tell me about your grandma.

J. A.   She loves me, but I'm naughty.

Dr. H.   What did you do?

J. A.   I hid in the closet. She can't find me.

Dr. H.   What happened?

J. A.   She called my dad.

Dr. H.   Then what happened?

J. A.   I got a spanking.

Dr. H.   Who spanked you?

J. A.   Daddy. Real hard.

Dr. H.   Are you naughty very much?

J. A.   No.

Dr. H.   Let's go back a little further and see what it is like when you were four years old. 1,2,3,4. You are four. Tell me what you are doing now.

J. A.   (Begins to cry) Nobody wanted me.

Dr. H.   Why didn't they want you? If you talk about it you will feel much better.

J. A.   (Sobs deeply).

Dr. H.   It's very hard for a little boy that's just four to feel this way, I know. But tell me about it and you will feel better. Where is your daddy?

J. A.   Gone.

Dr. H.   Where's grandma?

J. A.   I can't find her.

Dr. H.   Where are you living?

J. A.   The city.

Dr. H.   What town is it?

J. A.   I don't know.

Dr. H.   Where is your mother?

J. A.   She didn't want me.

Dr. H.   Who are you living with?

J. A.   Lots of places.

Dr. H.   Are they good to you? (Continues to sob.) Well, we'll not talk about it now — some other time. Let's go to a time when you were three. Go back until you are three years old, and tell me about it. Is it happier when you are three?

J. A.   No.

Dr. H.   Where are you living now?

138

J. A.   New Mexico

Dr. H.   Who are you living with in New Mexico?

J. A.   Grandma. We go to church.

Dr. H.   What are some of the other things you do?

J. A.   We just go to church.

Dr. H.   Now let's go back to the time you were two years old. Now you are two. Look around you and tell me what is happening.

J. A.   It's better.

Dr. H.   What's better?

J. A.   Grandpa is here. He loves me. He sings.

Dr. H.   What is he singing?

J. A.   Oh, dem golden slippers.

Dr. H.   What else does he sing?

J. A.   Ten little Indians. He plays the fiddle too.

Dr. H.   That is pretty good isn't it? So now we will go on back to one year—to the time you are one year old. Now you are one year old. Tell me exactly how you feel. and what's happening all around you. You will be able to speak about it as an adult, but you are actually living the experience as a baby one year old. (Began to cry, and then sob.) Tell me what is the matter.

J. A.   (More crying and sobbing.) I'm all alone.

Dr. H.   Where are you?

J. A.   In a room. I'm locked in.

Dr. H.   Who locked you in?

J. A.   Mother.

Dr. H.   Do you know where your mother went when she locked you in?

J. A.   No. I'm hungry. I'm on the floor. I'm crying.

Dr. H.   Have you been there long?

J. A.   Uh huh.

Dr. H.   Now let's go forward a little bit—until someone comes and unlocks the door. You will know who it is, and what they do and say. (Pause.) Who is it that comes in?

J. A.   My daddy. He picks me up. He loves me. He's holding me.

Dr. H.   What does he say to you?

J. A.   "Everything's going to be all right."

Dr. H.   Now you feel better. Now we're going back a little further to the time just before you were born. You are able to think about this as an adult, but you will be feeling everything just as you did when you originally went through it. As I count backward to zero you will be in the birth canal just about to be born. And you will know what it feels like. You will reexperience your birth, still thinking about it as an adult so that it does not upset you. One, zero. You are ready to be born. Tell me everything that is happening to you, and whether you are being born head first or feet first.

J. A.   Head.

Dr. H.   Now at the count of three the head will have been born, and you will feel a lot better. 1,2,3. Now your head is born. The body is not yet born. Tell me how you are feeling.

J. A.   Relaxed

Dr. H.   You are able to hear everything that is being said and to know everything that is going on in the room. As the birth progresses you will tell me everything that is happening and everything that is being said in the room.

J. A.   They're talking, but I can't hear.

140

Dr. H.   You're going to be able to hear it a little clearer with the count of three. 1,2,3. You are hearing plainer now. What are they saying? Who is in the room besides you and your mother?

J. A.   The doctor. He's young, blond. Mother's disappointed.

Dr. H.   Why is mother disappointed?

J. A.   I'm a boy.

Dr. H.   Did you hear her say this?

J. A.   Yes. She killed my brother.

Dr. H.   Did she say that?

J. A.   No.

Dr. H.   How do you know it?

J. A.   She didn't feed him.

Dr. H.   You know that even though you are just a newborn baby? (This would be knowing a fact which occurred before the present body was conceived, as well as knowing it at the time of birth.)

J. A.   Yes.

Dr. H.   (If a soul has a choice as to what body it will occupy, one might think that the soul would only choose the pleasant and happy situations. But the soul, apparently, does not operate on the pleasure-pain principle. It seeks to solve its karmic problems, to work out its own perfection.) Do you know why you came to this mother?

J. A.   No.

Dr. H.   Well, we can go back a little further — back to the time before birth, back to the time you will know why you are coming back to live this life. So go back in time until you come to the time when you have an awareness of the reason you are coming back into an earth experience

141

again. You will know why you are coming back to this particular mother and father. You will know and you will be able to tell me. So go back through time until the time of this decision. Now you know why you came to these parents. Why did you come?

J. A.   For my daddy.

Dr. H.   Had you known him before? (Usually the soul returns to those it has known before. This is often very necessary in order to continue to work out some special karmic problem.)

J. A.   Yes.

Dr. H.   Let us now go back to the time when you knew your daddy before. Your subconscious knows and it can search through your memory until it finds the time when you and this daddy were together before. When I reach the count of seven you will have found that time. 1,2,3,4,5,6,7. Look around you and tell me what is happening.

J. A.   He's my brother.

Dr. H.   Can you tell me the kind of house you live in?

J. A.   A log cabin.

Dr. H.   What part of the world are you living in?

J. A.   United States.

Dr. H.   Do you know what part?

J. A.   It's the country.

Dr. H.   Do you know the year it is?

J. A.   Seventeen and something.

Dr. H.   Tell me about your brother. What's his name?

J. A.   Jerry.

Dr. H.   Is he older or younger than you?

J. A.   He's sixteen.

Dr. H.   How old are you?

J. A.   Nearly seven. (Laughs.)

Dr. H.   What's happening?

J. A.   I'm dressed so funny. High-topped black shoes. Buttons on them. Fancy pants. A big straw hat on my head.

Dr. H.   Do you go to school?

J. A.   Yes, we write on slates.

Dr. H.   Let's go to school and have a lesson and tell me exactly what you are writing.

J. A.   It's arithmetic. Four times six.

Dr. H.   What's the answer?

J. A.   Twenty four.

Dr. H.   What happens if you get the wrong answer? Does the teacher scold you?

J. A.   Slaps you. Jerry's the only one who is good to me.

Dr. H.   Let's go back through time to see if there was another time when you and Jerry were together. Was there another time?

J. A.   He's a grown man.

Dr. H.   And you?

J. A.   I'm grown too. He's in uniform, a soldier.

Dr. H.   Do you know him well?

J. A.   He's my sweetheart.

Dr. H.   (Each soul, it is commonly believed, must experience life on earth in both male and female bodies. I have had reports of many such changes.) Would you like to marry him?

J. A.   Oh, yes.

Dr. H.   Are you able to get married to him?

J. A.   (Sadly.) No. He has to go to war.

Dr. H.   Does he come back from the war?

J. A.   No.

Dr. H.   What is your name?

J. A.   Kathleen Morris.

Dr. H.   Where are you living?

J. A.   In the south.

Dr. H.   What year is it?

J. A.   Civil war.

Dr. H.   Now we will go forward in time to the time when you have lived out that life as Kathleen and, just as a dream, you will be able to know the cause of the death and how long the life lasted. You are there now. Tell me what happened.

J. A.   I'm old, real old.

Dr. H.   How are you dressed?

J. A.   Like a witch, in gray.

Dr. H.   Did you ever get married in this life?

J. A.   No. He never came back.

Dr. H.   Now go forward until after this life has ended and you will be between lives. You will know how it happened that you left the body of Kathleen. Tell me what happened.

J. A.   I died of old age. Alone.

Dr. H.   There was no family at all?

J. A.   None. No one at all.

Dr. H.   Now you are betweeen lives. Tell me what is happening, how you feel, and what your thoughts are.

144

J. A.   It's better. I saw him.

Dr. H.   Your sweetheart?

J. A.   (Joyfully.) Yes.

Dr. H.   Are you with him now?

J. A.   (Ecstatically.) Yes.

Dr. H.   Now you are going forward in time to the time
         when you and Jerry were brothers; and then in-
         to your present life when he is your father. As I
         count to ten you will come forward all the way
         to the present. 1,2,3,4,5,6,7,8,9,10. You may
         wake up feeling very good. Wake up.

After Justin wakened, I asked him how he felt.

"Wonderful," he said, "But somehow I feel different.
What happened?"

He had no memory of what he had experienced. As he
listened to the tape recording the memory began to return.
His eyes had a far-away look. After hearing the tape he
remarked, "So that's why I have always felt so alone. I've
been alone for many lives."

I touched his hand. "That was a long time ago. Now that
you have reviewed this you can let go of that pattern and enjoy your life now. You are not alone now."

A smile crossed his face. "Thanks," he said, "very much."

His ulcers healed and did not recur. He was able to move
out and become more sociable. Within a year he was engaged
to be married. Both his health and his mood continued to improve.

It is surprising how many patients with long-existing
and serious problems are able to resolve them and return to
health after only a few hypnotic sessions.

The idea that psychotherapy, particularly
psychoanalysis must require years has certainly been
disproved by those of us who are using hypnosis.

One of the particularly satisfying cases concerned a girl
of age 18. Although she had a diploma from a California High
School, she was unable to read and comprehend even second
grade level reading material.

She was quickly hypnotized. When she was asked to go

back to the cause of her reading problem she began describing a scene of a quarrel between her mother and her father. Mother was calling father "stupid." Even though Nancy was only six years old she felt involved in the quarrel. She preferred her father, and made a vow at once to be like her father. Her words were, "If my father is stupid, then I will be stupid just like my father."

That was the beginning of her reading problem. She had kept her vow well. I helped her to see the quarrel scene from the eyes of a grown up girl of eighteen. She was able to see that it had been her choice to stop learning, and it could also be her choice to learn if she wanted to do so.

I spent only six sessions with her. At the end of this series, she was able to read, understand, and enjoy reading the Reader's Digest and other relatively uncomplicated reading matter.

Chapter 13

THE USE OF FANTASY AND FACT

"Thought convinces; feeling persuades.— If imagination furnishes the fact with wings, feeling is the great stout muscle which plies them and lifts him from the ground—Thought sees beauty: emotion feels it."
                                                        J.R. Lowell

Fantasy, it is often alleged, is an undesirable abberation—something to shun and avoid. Rational people, it is claimed, should stick with facts, not childish meaningless imaginings.

I find such claims to be without foundation. Fantasy is important and vital in our mental and emotional processes.

Whether it be the fantasy of sleep called dreams, or the imagery of the waking or hypnotized state, it is both normal and useful.

It is probably impossible to distinguish perfectly fact from fantasy in our waking life. When hypnosis is used, the material evoked is probably more factual than when we are in our normal waking consciousness. Inhibitions are deminished with hypnosis. There is less need to fantasize. There are fewer resistances— —much greater ability and willingness to report whatever is dredged up from the subconscious memory bank without distortion. When hypnosis is used a very intimate relationship develops between the subject and hypnotist. This heightens the element of trust allowing the subject to dare to be honest and direct.

Some of my subjects have in hypnosis produced fantasy scenes that proved to be just as useful in therapy as factual material from the recall of a real event. The fantasy details were used in the same way as non-fantasy, and with gratifying results.

M.C. was such a one. She was a recent widow in her mid-thirties. Her marriage had been very good. She blamed herself in part for her husbands sudden death. He had driven to the market to buy her candy just to satisy a whim. He was struck and killed as he walked out of the market, the box of candy in his hand. She felt that had she not asked for the candy he would still be alive.

Her transcript follows:

Dr. H.   What's happening?

M. C.   Huh . . . It's funny how you see things that you have talked about before. I see a mess, just like a mess of yarn all tangled up together, and all in different colors.

Dr. H.   Can you find an end?

M. C.   Seems like there are many reasons for it.

Dr. H.   What can you do with a tangled mess of yarn?

M. C.   You just start with one end and then wind.

Dr. H.   What happens if you just claw at it?

M. C.   Just gets more messed up.

Dr. H.   Let's find an end. You turn it over and look all around until you find an end. Tell me the color as you start to wind. Follow this color. Make a little ball of it and loop it over and under and through the mess until you get it all straightened out.

M. C.   I can't find an end. It's an awful mess.

Dr. H.   Well, you keep turning it over. You'll find an end in a moment.

M. C.   It's yellow.

Dr. H.   Start winding up this yellow strand and as you wind you will come to realize what it stands for. (Deep puzzlement crossed her face.) What's happening? Are you getting it untangled a bit?

M. C.   It looks like sunshine.

Dr. H.   Are you still winding the yellow

M. C.   It means happiness.

Dr. H.   So you find sunshine and happiness as the first part of your tangled mess. Are there any other meanings?

M. C.   I keep seeing flashes of happy times.

Dr. H.   Do you want to talk about some of these happy times? You can talk and wind at the same time. Tell me whatever flashes you come to.

M. C.   Oh, just how very, very happy I was when I was married. Complete, just a feeling of oneness. I never had that feeling with anyone else. When I talk about it, it makes me sad.

Dr. H.   Are you still winding yellow?

M. C.   (Long pause.) No, black.

Dr. H.   Then wind the black a little bit. If any flashes come, tell me about them. Talk while you wind. What are you feeling now?

M. C.   Oh, I don't know. I guess I could cry and cry forever.

Dr. H.   You could cry for half a minute and it would feel like you had cried forever. Let it pour out until you have cried it all out—in about half a minute. Keeping it inside causes a kind of emotional constipation, you know.

M. C.   But everybody says you should be strong, you shouldn't cry.

Dr. H.   Who is the everybody that says this?

M. C.   Oh, at the office and my in-laws.

Dr. H.   Just let yourself cry for a few seconds and you'll feel as if you had cried it all out. You don't need to fight it here. Express your real feelings at all times. When you have cried it all out you

149

will find that the color of the yarn has changed. (Deep sobs for about twenty seconds.) Feeling better? What color are you winding now?

M. C.   Blue. I see my little boy at various stages of his development.

Dr. H.   Blue often has to do with intellectual things. Does it now have to do with his learning, growing up and experiencing new things?

M. C.   It isn't clear. I just see flashes of him.

Dr. H.   (After a long pause) What's happening now?

M. C.   It's red.

Dr. H.   What do you see while you wind the red?

M. C.   My health. If I could only get my health straightened out. But it's all intertwined. All these things affect the whole.

Dr. H.   These aren't separate strands at all, are they? They are one long piece of yarn in every color—all the same strand.

M. C.   Yes. I just don't have the confidence that I need to get in there and straighten it all out.

Dr. H.   Is this discouraging?

M. C.   Yes.

Dr. H.   Let's just keep on winding and maybe you'll see how it became so tangled.

M. C.   I just see words, words all around everywhere.

Dr. H.   Just call them out and they'll begin to line up and make sense to you.

M. C.   They are all the things that plague me, I guess.

Dr. H.   What are they?

M. C.   Indigestion, dizziness, weight.

Dr. H.   Is this why you are winding the red—because these are the things that anger you?

THE USE OF FANTASY AND FACT

M. C.   Insecurity, responsibility . . . . . .

Dr. H.   Call off each word.

M. C.   Depression, hopelessness, despair, unhap-
piness, lonliness.

Dr. H.   Is that all?

M. C.   Frustration—I want so badly to do something
about it all and it seems that everywhere I start
it just makes a worse tangled mess.

Dr. H.   Let's wind some more. I'll help you. We'll un-
tangle it some more. I'll pull a little bit, so you
can wind it more easily. What color is it now?

M. C.   Pink. This is a little glimmer of hope.

Dr. H.   I'll help you some more, so you can find where
the pink strand goes. Do you see it?

M. C.   Only a little . . . . .

Dr. H.   Keep winding. It goes faster as you wind.

M. C.   If I could just find success with one thing, then
maybe I'd have confidence. I just feel that I'm in
a maze and just run and run and run.

Dr. H.   Maybe it would be better if you would slow
down. Let your feelings out.

M. C.   There is no way out. It's closing in on me. It's
worse and worse.

Dr. H.   You are finding your way out. Keep winding the
tangled yarn. Each turn as you wind it will
make less entanglement. What color are you
winding now?

M. C.   Green.

Dr. H.   Good, good. As you wind you will know what
the green means.

M. C.   It won't come. I don't see anything.

Dr. H.   Let's not try to force it. Let you subconscious
mind show you. Sometimes we have to be

patient no matter how anxious we are to get it over with. The harder we pull the more the yarn tangles. Just be patient. First undo this knot and then the next.

M. C.   It won't budge.

Dr. H.   Let's ask your subconscious mind to show you what kind of tool you need to continue with this winding. What kind of tool do you need to help with the knots?

M. C.   The thing that comes is self-discipline.

Dr. H.   Let's ask your subconscious mind to show you the effect of self-discipline. Let's apply a little self-disciplining lubricant, or whatever is necessary, to this tangled skein. Now let your subconscious show you the results that would take place with the self-discipline properly applied. Does that help you to go on winding?

M. C.   Then the green comes easily. There's a lot of green in there but it comes slowly. There are other forces that keep pulling at me.
(At this point she began to speak of herself as 'she' and seemed to be viewing the scene from the viewpoint of a spectator.)
She feels pulled in all directions, but she's learning what it's all about. She really is resolved to work out her problems. She's still winding the green, but she does feel much better.

Dr. H.   How does the tangled yarn look now?

M. C.   There's long pieces sticking out — it's smaller. It looks a lot better.

Dr. H.   How much remains tangled?

M. C.   About a fourth.

This was a most useful fantasy using the tangled skein symbol. As she straightened out her skein of yarn — what she called the "mess of my life" — the fantasy tangle likewise became free and each color became wound up on neat balls that she could handle.

Larry Peters (another fictional name) also used fantasy creations to explain himself to himself. At thirty, he considered himself a total failure. He had left his employment with a religious organization just before being fired. He felt very sorry for himself. There was nothing he enjoyed doing. Life looked pretty discouraging. It was the third session before I found even one thing that gave him pleasure. Following is a transcript of that third session:

L. P.   I like to go watch the water.

Dr. H.   All right, just think of yourself now as watching the water — just growing quieter and quieter — just thinking of nothing but the water flowing along.

L. P.   The trouble is a lot of times the guys would say that's silly, you know — let's be practical.

Dr. H.   It may be silly there with them, but here it isn't silly. It is the thing to do. Just let your subconscious bring up whatever it wants to show you. Nothing is silly.

L. P.   Um-hum I see a big giant.

Dr. H.   Tell me about him.

L. P.   He's standing over the river. A great big giant.

Dr. H.   Go on, tell me about the giant.

L. P.   I don't know. He's just a big giant. He's just standing there.

Dr. H.   Is this some sort of dream?

L. P.   Yes, it's just what I am going to do. I know what this is all about — you just dream, you know. It doesn't make any difference if it sounds crazy?

Dr. H.   No. We can have crazy dreams if we want to.

L. P.   Well, it's a big giant, ha-ha-ha. He's funny too, I think. (Almost child-like voice) I'm going to tackle him — he's going to fall. That's what I did to my brother once, ha-ha-ha. He's a big guy — weighs over two hundred pounds, and all that kind of stuff. He was chasing me once in the yard and I don't know how I just turned around and charged him. Caught him around the ankles and boy! Did he fall hard! Ha-ha-ha.

Dr. H.　How old were you then?

L. P.　Just teenage kids, I guess. (More laughter.)

Dr. H.　You catch him by surprise and then he falls flat?

L. P.　Yes, he does. I don't let him chase me — I sneak up on him. He tries to scare me, but I surprise him. When I'm sitting by the river, looking at the river he tries to scare me, or something. It's just the way I felt when I was at the river yesterday. I felt somebody was going to come and tell me to get out of there.

Dr. H.　Did they?

L. P.　No — I kept the doors locked in the car so they couldn't get in. That was kind of silly.

Dr. H.　Anything is all right so long as you are not doing any harm to anyone. It's all right to be silly if you want to be silly.

L. P.　I can just still see the giant. He just stands still. I can't see his face very good. He's just astraddle of the river.

Dr. H.　What kind of garments is he wearing?

L. P.　Kind of like Robin Hood. (Laughing.) He can't get me. He can't get me. I have the car locked. I think he's getting mad 'cause he can't move.

Dr. H.　Why can't he move?

L. P.　I think it's because maybe his feet are chained down, or something, to the sides of the river, or banks. He's standing clear up across the river, with his legs spread out on either side, and I think they are ... well, I think they're stuck or chained. Or they look like they've got big bands over them or screwed down or something. (More laughter.)

Dr. H.   He can't do anything?

L. P.   He can't move. No. I just laugh at him.

Dr. H.   What does the giant represent?

L. P.   Well, I don't know.

Dr. H.   Just listen to the inner voice.

L. P.   Well, he—ah—well, he's just a big dumb guy, you know.

Dr. H.   What meaning does he have for you?

L. P.   Well, he kind of clouds up the horizon. I want to watch the river and he just messes up the landscape. (Laughter.) That's all—he just messes up the landscape. There goes a boat down, a tug boat pulling a barge, and it has airplanes on it. That's what I see. I like to watch boats.

Dr. H.   As you watch them you become quieter and quieter. You can hear more clearly the inner voice. You are more and more quiet, more and more drowsy. Just let yourself take a nap as you sit there watching the river.

L. P.   The boat just goes right between his legs and on down the river. (Laughter.) They don't even know he is there. They can't see him. I can see him though. He's getting mad—oh, he's mad!

Dr. H.   How does he show his anger?

L. P.   Oh, he just . . . He's trying to pull his feet out and they are stuck.

Dr. H.   Do you ever feel like this?

L. P.   Oh, God, yes.

Dr. H.   Let's talk a little about this feeling.

L. P.   Oh, oh, it's awful, just awful, He can't move.

Dr. H.   Well, let's ask the inner voice what can be done.

L. P.   Oh, I'll just yank my feet up out of the mud, that's what I'll do, damn it. They're just in the mud anyhow and those . . . . .

Dr. H.   They're now chained?

L. P.   No, they're not chained. They're, they have these kind of staples — big — huge — jammed down over the shoes into the ground. But all you have to do is yank your foot up and it comes right out.

Dr. H.   What are the staples like?

L. P.   Well, my father pounded them in there when the giant wasn't looking or somebody did. They pounded them down and they told him that they wouldn't — or he thought they wouldn't come up or something. I don't know. Maybe the ground was dry and they wouldn't.

Dr. H.   So he can't pull his feet loose?

L. P.   Yea, it's like mud. If he wants to, the darned nut. He's so darn dumb, though. (Laughing.) I think he'd rather stay there with them stuck in the mud.

Dr. H.   How do you feel about this giant standing there, and staying stuck in the mud instead of pulling his feet out and going on?

L. P.   (Laughing hard.) He's funny.

Dr. H.   Ridiculous, isn't it?

L. P.   Oh, dumb nut.

Dr. H.   What's the giant's name?

L. P.   Oh, fuddydud.

Dr. H.   What's his real name?

L. P.   (Evading.) Isn't me — don't tell me it's me.

Dr. H.　I'm not telling you. I'm asking you. What's his real name?

L. P.　His name is Mr. Unreasonable Fear. That's who he is. You know he looks terrible. And he tries to scare everybody that sees him. That tugboat captain doesn't see him. He's not afraid of him.

Dr. H.　He's Mr. Unreasonable Fear? You're rather well acquainted with him, aren't you?

L. P.　Oh, God, yes. Oh, I got frightened when I woke up this morning . . . . . just scared to death.

Dr. H.　Maybe he needs to get himself a new name.

L. P.　(Laughing.) I'll just tackle him and make him go splash in the water, that's what I'll do. Get him all wet.

Dr. H.　Will that get his feet loose?

L. P.　Well, they might come loose when he hits the water. (More laughter.)

Dr. H.　Let's try it.

L. P.　I just pushed him over. (More laughing.)

Dr. H.　Did you?

L. P.　Yea, sure I pushed him over. He hit the water with a big splash. His feet are still stuck in the mud. He's so big that he's just sitting in the water, though its deep. (Laughter.)

Dr. H.　Watch him a while. See if he can get his feet loose.

L. P.　Yeah, he's got 'em loose now. He's sitting over there in the mud. He sure is a mess over there on that side of the bank. Sitting in the mud — he's lost all his dignity now.

Dr. H.　Does he know he is loose?

L. P.　Yeah, and he's not puffed up any more. He's just sitting there in the mud . . . kind of whipped. He's trying to scare little boys, or something, and he got put in his place. (Laughing.)

Dr. H.   What is he doing now?

L. P.   He looks so stupid sitting there. He's funny, you
           know. You can laugh at him . . . he's just all beat
           out. He's shrinking. Just like a balloon — s-s-s-s,
           he's going down. He's just a tiny thing now . . . .
           a tiny doll. The sun's coming out now nice and
           warm.

With the giant standing astride the river indentified as
Mr. Unreasonable Fear, and then put in his place, and the promise of a nice warm sun, Larry began to get to the factual
material of his problem. He had always been playing the part
of the Big Shot, but like the giant, he was frequently deflated.
He began to understand this and to understand that there
were things more wonderful and important than money and
position. A portion of a later session transcript follows:

L. P.   Well, you know, being on this right path now, I
           think of music, and poetry and art and walking
           by the seashore.

Dr. H.   So you don't have a million dollars . . . . does it
           matter?

L. P.   I just feel like I was in a different world. I
           remember when I was going to college. My wife
           and I used to take a day off and go over to the
           coast and walk along the beach . . . even if it was
           raining or not. I used to talk to her, and tell her
           how scientists would destroy the song of the
           bird when they dissected it. In college we were
           always dissecting everything. I always said
           there was more — there's got to be more — than
           that. You tear everything apart, and there's not
           a damned thing left. You analyze God till God is
           phsst! He's gone and you can't hear the song of
           the bird, and you can't hear the music in the
           waves. I didn't get any of that in college and I
           was starved for it. It was all analyze, analyze,
           analyze . . . Do you know what I mean?

Dr. H.   Everything was completely intellectual?

L. P.   Oh, God, you can't let yourself go along and just listen to what you hear. Maybe I'm a nut or something. Maybe there isn't any music in the waves.

Dr. H.   There is a long as you feel there is.

As Larry pushed the giant into the water, he started on the road toward the solutions to his problems. Mr. Unreasonable Fear had kept him locked in a panic state. As he tackled the terrible-looking giant again and again the giant was completely vanquished.

Mr. Unreasonable Fear, a fearful and shadowy creation of Larry Peters' mind was the horrible symbol of his almost unbearable burden. He first met and recognized Mr. Unreasonable Fear when under hypnosis. We could now treat him as a fact. We did not attempt to explain him away. For Larry he was indeed a reality.

So many people who register confusion or lack of insight about their problems, make amazing discoveries through the use of hypnosis.

The statements they make when hypnotized frequently show the deepest insights, not only into the nature and source of their problems, but also often contain profound wisdom.

It continues to amaze me that this level of wisdom is repeatedly produced by folks whose waking life is so tangled and unsatisfactory. In this regard there is no disagreement. The material produced while hypnotized is harmonious with that produced by other patients, even though when awake the diversity would be wide.

Mary Hunter was such a one, who was seeming far wiser when asleep than when awake.

She was in her forties, twice divorced, and searching for a deeper meaning to her life. Here is an excerpt from one of her sessions.

M. H.   Just practice what you preach. I have to make up my mind that my neurosis can either be an asset or a liability. (Then seeming to carry on an argument with herself.) How can a neurosis be an asset? You have to get rid of them. That's silly.

Dr. H.   What's silly?

M. H.   Neurotic people. The more intelligent, the more neurotic —seems like that's what comes out. A neurosis is but a neurotic drive - the force of an individual that must do things . . . . accomplish things. Actually you can take neurotic people, very neurotic people, and you can accomplish very great things with them, or they can destroy themselves and others. They can go either way. You can use these forces for good or bad. The neurotic drive and this tremendous desire to do things can be used either way. But the individual must have the desire to channel them along the good, and then they will stay more on that side than the other. But being neurotic, they will always have some evidence of both. They usually don't fail. They make a success no matter which way they go. They can go to the good and make a success, or they can go to the bad and really make a success of it. They can really foul their lives up. They go to extremes. They don't have to but they have to have a purpose, or a reason, a goal, or a direction, a guide to work in line with.

M. H.   (Later in the same session.) There's such a bright—real bright beam of light. It's a real, real bright beam of light, and it's coming in this direction and going that way (gesturing from left to right.) It's just a bright feeling, real bright. I see the words start coming. At the first there is 'Vesuvius,' and then 'Geruvius,' and then 'Genesis.' Genesis, thirteen, twelve. I don't know what they mean. Seems to have something to do with the Bible, but I don't know anything about Genesis, or anything like that. The light—the book is open and there is some red writing.

Dr. H.   We'll get up closer to it and you will be able to

read it. I'll help you by counting from one to five. One, two, three, four, five. Now you can read it.

M. H.   Everybody knows what that means but it wouldn't be in the Bible, I don't think. It says, I don't understand it, it says, 'Paternostrum,' and 'E pluribus unum.' It's Latin, but I don't know what it means. I don't know why all these Biblical words and names keep coming out. I don't know anything about such things—

A few more of the disconnected phrases and then a lengthy description of a man and woman walking along a jungle path. Then she saw a negro couple in Africa who were hiding from the rest of the tribe. The man was tender with the woman and picked a flower and put it in her hair.

M. H.   . . . There's that funny noise again.

Dr. H.   Why is there a funny noise?

M. H.   Because I won't listen.

Dr. H.   Then listen for a little while and you will learn something which will help you understand your problem.

M. H.   It's too silly. 'Speak out . . . Hold true thy trust.' It sounds like a prayer. 'Ever be gentle. I am at your side.'

Dr. H.   Where are these words coming from?

M. H.   I don't know.

After a few more sessions, M. H. reported that the source of the visual scenes and the words was from her own subconscious mind. They proved to have significant meaning for her. As is often true with dreams, there may have been more meaning there than we had elicited. She found the answers that she needed at the time.

The subconscious mind sometimes uses disguised material in what appears to be an effort to overcome the patient's resistance. When the language of the symbols is understood, the information becomes helpful and useful.

Fantasy material is uncommon. When it is produced, it can be used in ways to help the subject gain insights, allowing them to straighten out the tangled skein of their lives, or master an emotion, or understand their strong urges and feelings.

The benefits of using fantasy can be equal to the use of other hypnotherapy techniques. They include improved physical health, a greater emotional freedom, improved personal relationships, a more satisfactory marriage, greater creativity or deeper spiritual awareness.

Chapter 14

PROBING - - - - HOW DEEP?

"The more accurately we search into the human mind, the stronger traces we everywhere find of the wisdom of Him who made it."   Edmund Burke

Critics of hypnosis raise a number of questions. Is hypnosis subject to scientific testing? Can we really determine hypnotizability? Is the information obtained valid? Is the hypnotized subject unduly influenced by the hypnotist?

There remain vast areas to be tested. It is my hope that scientifically trained people proceed to apply old and new test methods to hypnosis and find out all the ways it can be helpful—to really probe the human mind. This would be the next great adventure—exploring a largely unexplored universe.

In the area of childbirth alone, where hypnosis is more widely used than in other medical departments, there is still much that is not understood. Just how useful is hypnosis in easing the pain of childbirth? Are there other benefits beyond pain relief. Does the use of hypnosis diminish the need for surgical intervention? Does it give the doctor greater control? Does it shorten the length of labor? Does it diminish the fatigue of the mother? Does is allow a more joyous response of the mother? Does it benefit the baby?

Perhaps a more widespread use of hypnosis for childbirth might reduce or eliminate the thousands of cases of severe brain damage which result every year. Other possible advantages might be discovered.

Even without this added data, the advantages of hypnoanesthesia so far outweigh the disadvatages, that I react with annoyance and appalled perplexity that doctors still use dangerous drugs to ease the pain of labor. It raises the question of whether they are practicing their profession in a way that the patients have a right to expect. Any new drug that could offer the benefits of hypnosis would be hailed as a miracle-of-miracles drug.

We do not know the extent to which hypnosis is used for anesthesia in minor or major surgery or dentistry. It would be helpful for researchers to collect data on what is being done, and then to analyze the data. If it would become widely known that hypnosis is being used extensively and with wide benefits, perhaps the more hesitant medical practitioners would be encouraged to also begin to use this safe, simple and valuable tool.

My primary interest, however, concerns research into the use of hypnosis in psychosomatic cases. This would be more difficult, of course, but ultimately, I believe, could prove to be the most valuable. Perhaps hypnosis properly used could eliminate the need for the thousands of prescriptions for tranquilizers sold every day. Real research could demonstrate unmistakeably whether there is benefit or not, and the extent of the benefit or possible harm.

In psychotherapy, in education, in law-enforcement, in rehabilitation, in sports, in creative arts or just in living abundantly, how much can this tool, hypnosis, help? In the Spring Semester of 1981 at Northeast Missouri State University, two senior psychology majors ran a research project comparing the relaxation benefits of hypnosis to that of biofeedback. Their observations indicated that hypnotized subjects were far more deeply relaxed than were the biofeedback subjects or the controls.

I am not a researcher. I do not have the proper temperament for it. It takes a special type of person for research. I do not fit that mold. I am a therapist and a teacher. My interest is in the patient, not the method. I want to see him or her get well by whatever method I may call upon. I often wish that I were more concerned with research, for I know its great value. I see the incredible lack of research in my particular field of work.

There are so many applications or potential applications for which we have little information. We do have some sensational claims based on only a few instances. Frequently the sensationalism of these claims has repelled more people than it has attracted.

It would be valuable to pursue increasing uses of hypnosis in the law enforcement field. Just how accurately and completely is it possible to reconstruct a crime by hypnotizing the witnesses?

Another possible use of hypnosis might be to tap the seldom used potentials of the mind. Perhaps hypnosis could be used to find lost articles, minerals deposits, missing persons and the like. Unconfirmed reports have claimed fantastic results in this area. These claims may be exaggerated. I would like to see this possibility adequately investigated. There are, I believe, untapped abilities of the human mind—perhaps treasures beyond our most optimistic dreams. Exploring for this information could be a great adventure.

Perhaps many others have the talent of Edgar Cayce, an uneducated man who when hypnotized and when asked gave medical diagnoses and recommended treatment for the sick. He also stated that others could do the same thing that he did. We cannot prove or disprove this until we test the idea properly. We cannot know the answers until first we ask the questions. This is an area relatively easy to research and is subject to scientific control. Physicians could promptly verify or refute whatever a hypnotic subject would say regarding medical diagnosis. This would be without risk to the patients, and with possible great benefit. Edgar Cayce reported a great number of diagnoses that had been missed by skilled physicians. There is a stong probability that others with Edgar Cayce's ability could be found and developed.

My own excursions into this area were few, but they were encouraging. My few findings do not constitute proof. They only suggest that an exciting project is possible. I would like to see carefully controlled research in this area. Diagnosis is the most difficult of all medical problems. Once diagnosis is certain, treatment may be procedural and often simple. Patients suffer, and sometimes die, while waiting for the doctor to find out what is wrong.

In my office, psychotherapy proceeds on the presumption that the subconscious mind knows the nature, the cause and the remedy for all problems. When asked directly, the subconscious mind will bring forth the information. This subconscious knowledge includes both physical and psychological problems. Hypnotized persons in touch with their own subconscious have this information available to them.

However, according to Edgar Cayce, he could tune in to the subconscious level of another person and bring out seemingly unlimited volumes of information. Perhaps Cayce's work can be replicated by others if we only make the attempt.

One small example of this kind of latent talent was exhibited by Lois O., an excellent subject without medical background. She was interested in hypnosis and in the possibilities of it. She wanted to know whether she could do things under hypnosis beyond that possible without hypnosis. She consented to participate in a small experiment more out of curiosity than because she expected positive results. When she was deeply hypnotized, I asked her to examine the body of Edith W., a patient with multiple confusing symptoms and complaints.

L. O.   Well, this is somethng I hear. I hear her saying, 'Why do I have to hear that?' This was a long time ago. Must be her mother and her grandmother arguing and she walks in. The argument upsets her. She gets sick to her stomach, and it is hard for her to eat. She dislikes her grandmother, or did, but she could never say it. That was wrong. She thought her grandmother was mean. There is a little girl walking into a room. She sasses this grandmother. The grandmother said something to her and reached out and slapped her in the face. It made her ears ring, and her face burn. Sometimes people who can't see, don't want to see. (Poor sight and hearing were complaints of Edith.) This applies to hearing too. She's not deaf, she just doesn't hear. She interrupts the hearing process with noise whenever anything starts to get unpleasant. It's one way of shutting it out-to escape.

Dr. H.   How old was she when she got slapped?

L. O.   Seems like five. I see a flowered pattern of

166

linoleum, blue background and flowers on the border. Not much furniture—kind of old fashioned like—and a bed, an iron bed, a real old fashioned iron bed. There's somebody sitting in a chair. It might be a wheel chair, I don't know. The little girl's walking and she's looking back and she trips over something. Somebody calls her clumsy brat—stupid, clumsy brat. She is tall and thin. There are windows. There's a bed and to the right of the bed there are windows, three front windows. Might be a bay window. There's a wooden rocking chair, dark wood, with rungs in the back. She sits down and rocks in it and she's told to stop. Seems as though everybody's sick. There's a pot-bellied black stove. It's smoked up. This is a room she should remember. (Edith W. stated that this was a most accurate description.)

Dr. H. Go on. Tell whatever you see.

L. O. It was during this time that this trouble started. Began with her ears, and she cried herself to sleep, and was hurt by the things said to her. When she cried they would say, 'Well, cry again," and she would hold her crying until she went to bed, and then she would cry herself to sleep. This is one reason she has trouble now when she goes to bed. Conditioned reflexes from past anxiety. All the feeling connected with these experiences hasn't been expended. She tenses and holds her muscles tight. She doesn't relax . . . the muscle tones are not proper . . . improper uses. Did she ask about constipation?

Dr. H. Yes, that's right.

L. O. I didn't know she had trouble like that. Well, if she will look back to when she was a little girl, she used to always make a horrible face when she would be trying to go to the bathroom. From the time she was a little girl, she used the wrong set of muscles, so they became lax and weak and improperly trained in the bowel tract. She was using her face and stomach muscles, and everything else. She should have been corrected then. She used the wrong muscles to defecate. That sound silly, but that's the way it was. And, oh, also the body functions have always been referred to as something bad. Everything's bad, nasty and dirty. These problems are not all physical. I hear someone saying, 'Did you wash you hands? Go right back and wash your hands.' She says, 'My hands aren't dirty.' But they say, 'Wash your hands before you touch that!' Somebody is fanatic about it. So stern. She just kind of draws within herself, her little shell. She didn't rebel back. She was submissive, and she built up a protective wall which nobody could pierce. Of course she forgets that she built the wall so thick that no one could get through to her and she couldn't get out either. It was almost like a prison. (At this point Edith was brought into the room.)

Dr. H. Edith is here now. You will be able to hear Edith's voice, and when she asks a question, you will be able to hear it and answer it.

E. W. Why do I fear knives so?

L. O. She was told not to handle knives or she would cut herself. Just go back to when she was little, when she was trying to cut something with a knife, and it slipped out of her hand. Somebody said, 'I told you not to do that. You'll get hurt!' There is also something here about a bottle. She has hold of a broken glass. Doesn't seem to be a baby bottle. Maybe it was broken, or she broke it, and she's trying to clean it up before they catch her. (There followed more discussion of how she could break this emotional habit of fearing knives and broken glass.)

Dr. H. Why is she afraid of men?

L. O.   She is fearing herself more than men. Basically she is warm inside, affectionate and loving, but it doesn't come out. She has built this wall to keep people out and it keeps her in. She is afraid of herself, and what others will say. What they think or say doesn't matter, she should know. (For several minutes Lois lectured Edith about learning to love herself so others could love her too.)

Dr. H.   Will you now examine the physical body of Edith and see if there are any abnormalities. She describes a lump in her right side. Give the cause and any helpful treatment to remedy the condition.

L. O.   She won't like this at all, but it is strictly unrequited love and guilt feelings. She has to hurt. Small lump up under the rib on the right side. If examined by a doctor, they would not notice the lump necessarily.

Dr. H.   Is Edith able to feel some of her normal internal organs and think that they are abnormal?

L. O.   Yes, but in the colon, there's . . . there's a pocket, maybe a degree of diverticulosis, or diverticulitis, inflammation. Many people live prfectly normal lives with this condition. Many people have it in small amounts, but they never are bothered with it. I guess they do. That's what I'm saying. (More discussion of several of Edith's emotional problems, which seemed to cause most of her physical problems.)

Dr. H.   She says she is deaf in the left ear.

L. O.   That's still psychosomatic. It's a condition she has brought upon herself. Now there is a physical defect because of what started out as psychosomatic. My suggestion is that she be given a hearing test under hypnosis, and then the suggestion that she can hear perfectly well in that ear. If she can hear with it under hypnosis, she can hear with it when she's out too.

Dr. H.   One more thing— she sometimes has spells of roaring in her ears.

L. O.   She'll get the answer to that herself under hypnosis.

Dr. H.   Is she trying to find out these things for herself right now?

L. O.   Well, she has a way of hedging. You may fool a lot of people but you don't fool yourself at all.

This diagnosis had been amazingly accurate. Both Edith and I were astonished by much of it. But most surprised of all was Lois O. She had no memory of her words in the hypnotic trance. She listened to the tape in a state of awe. She could not believe that she had produced accurate information about someone else, and had shown knowledge about events and conditions beyond normal knowledge.

I wish I could have continued this kind of work with Lois O., but circumstances separated us soon after this experiment. I feel sure that she had the potential to do much more trance diagnoses. Such a person could be a wonderful aid to any doctor, simplifying the most difficult tasks of finding the nature of patients problems. Perhaps this faculty of at least some minds could provide services for patients which are now unavailable. The possibility merits serious attention and investigation.

Perhaps the most difficult area of hypnosis research has to do with reincarnation. It is not difficult to gather information. Hypnotized subjects readily give extensive information in detail about former lives. Names, addresses, dates, scene descriptions are all easily obtained.

The best known such case was *Bridey Murphey* told by author Morey Bernstein in *The Search for Bridey Murphey*, which was first published in 1956. This book told of a Colorado housewife who, when hypnotized, reported being named Bridey Murphey in Ireland in the early 1800's. She gave a great many details of her former life in Ireland, details later checked by the late Bill Barker, then a reporter for the Denver Post. Barker went to Ireland and found numerous obscure details which seemed to support the Bridey Murphey story. Not all details were supported, however. Both believers and non-believers found comfort in the partial verification.

My own opinion is that all that was demonstrated here was that a Colorado woman when hypnotized could give details, some of which could be verified, about a person who lived in another country 150 years earlier. Even if every tiny detail could have been verified, it would not prove to me that one was the reincarnation of the other. Nor would the absence of verification of even one detail disprove anything.

Since I am not personally impressed by this kind of evidence, I have made no effort to check out the details elicited from my patients. My interest is in helping the ill, the troubled, the confused — not to collect and check details.

For those who are interested, this could constitute a field of research. There is an organization The Association for Past-Life Research and Therapy, P.O. Box 20151, Riverside California, which is indeed in this kind of work. I applaud their efforts.

To those who have already closed their minds to the idea of reincarnation, proof must be submitted in the manner they prescribe. Even if material is verifiable 100%, they then claim that it is all material which the subject could have learned in this life. However unlikely such learning may have been, there is always a possibility. I do not deny the possibility, but do see the possession of obscure or highly technical details by persons of limited education or experience as strong evidence for its validity.

Additional problems arise when material reported is from an ancient time and cannot be verified. This adds comfort to the critics. Their position is uncontestable. It appears that the material is from the imagination of the subject. The idea of past lives can be rejected whether or not the details can be verified. With confirmed non-believers, no discussion of possible past lives is possible.

A better way that verifying reported details from former lives would be to check cross references. Almost every patient giving past life material reports their former life included someone known to them in this life. If true, then the other persons should be able to recall the same details from their own point of view.

This may not always be successful for a variety of reasons. My feeling is that the failures are of little significance. My interest is in what data can be collected that can be checked against itself. My curiosity is concerned with what is possible to find as we wander through the vast unexplored territory of our minds. I find this kind of exploration to contain endless variety and excitement. Each mind is as vast as a new unexplored continent—full of surprises and challenges, and able to provide answers to riddles that have perplexes sages throughout history.

When successful—when two or more people do recall the same material, this seems to me to be very strong evidence. When done independently and in careful detail, the evidence cannot be totally ignored.

This has happened in my experience on several occasions, but never with adequate controls. I would like to see an experiment with rigid controls. One possible good structure would be to have the subjects in separate rooms, each hypnotized by separate hypnotists, who preferably were strangers to each other, and to eliminate all contact between them during the experiments. It would also be helpful to have the hypnotists strangers to the opposite subject. When either hypnotist regressed the subject to a past life event in which the opposite subject was present, only the date or place information would be relayed to the other team. If this is done and both subjects go on to relate compatible material, the evidence is potent. If this were repeated through several episodes, the evidence becomes more convincing. Such evidence indicates either the factuality of past lives, or the existence of a communication level between minds in this life which could inspire further investigation.

Two patients of mine, sisters, Judy and Kate Monroe (fictional names) came to me with complaints of multiple fears and psychosomatic ailments. They were in their late thirties. Neither had ever been married and had lived together all their lives. I first worked with them in separate sessions during which they each went back to similar scenes. I then hypnotized them together, to deal them simultaneously.

This is what occurred the first time we did this:

Dr. H.	(To Judy) Have you found a time when you and the person now your sister, Kate, were together before?
J. M.	Well, I feel very close to her.
Dr. H.	(To Kate.) Have you found such a time?
K. M.	Not yet.
Dr. H.	Tell me what's happening, Judy.
J. M.	I seem to go back to . . . I don't know . . . It's not clear. (Pause.) It seems like . . . it was when I was is Holland. This was when my husband passed away. I was grieving so. This person was very close to me.
Dr. H.	Find a time when you are having a conversation with this person. What are you saying?
J. M.	Well, oh-oh-oh . . .
Dr. H.	What's being said?
J. M.	It was my husband's sister. I went to stay with her. She was very kind to me. She wanted to know what I was going to do now, and if I wanted to stay with her.
Dr. H.	What did you tell her?
J. M.	Well, I didn't care to stay alone, and I would like to stay with her, if she had room.
Dr. H.	Now, you can hear the sounds of the words as this conversation is taking place. Repeat exactly the words you spoke, and the words she spoke, and then you will give me the meaning in English.
J. M.	(Speaking in what sounded like a foreign language and then translating.) Well, I say . . . Well, I'm not very happy now. I'm feeling pretty bad because of the loss of my husband. She will make room for me in her little place. I don't like to give up my home, but I don't want to live alone, my folks are far away. She's the only one

near.

Dr. H. (To Kate.) Kate, have you found the time that we are talking about? Is it familiar to you?

K. M. A little bit.

Dr. H. What's happening as you see it?

K. M. I just feel very happy inside that she's going to live with us.

J. M. She has two children.

K. M. But they won't disturb her.

J. M. They are ten and thirteen. Nice children. I'll be happier there than staying alone. Oh, her husband. It's going to make me miss mine so. I didn't get to have a baby. I'm sorry, so sorry.

Dr. H. (To Kate.) Tell me more about it as you see it.

K. M. Well I felt so bad losing my brother. Just as bad as she did. I loved him. But I gained a sister-in-law.

Dr. H. Continue your conversation with you sister-in-law.

K. M. (To Judy) Oh, darling, you'll be so much happier living with us. Even if you do miss him, you'll be happy here. (Began speaking in the foreign sounding tongue, which sounded Dutch, but which I never officially verified.) I do know you miss him. He has gone to his reward.

Dr. H. (To Kate.) What is your name?

K. M. Greta.

Dr. H. All right, Greta, continue your conversation with your sister-in-law.

K. M. (More foreign tongue.) We'll have fun together. I have always wanted a sister, and never had one. (More foreign tongue.)

Dr. H. (To Judy.) Now you have been hearing what your sister-in-law, Greta, has been saying. You will answer just as she has been speaking.

J. M.   We . . .we are both very emotional right now. She's as emotional as I am. (Same presumed foreign tongue . .)

I did not have this language identified or translated. I cannot be certain it was a language, but it appeared to me to have all the characteristics of a language.

There were several sessions during which these two sisters relived their sister-in-law relationship in Holland, and spoke to each other in that other language.

Another interesting case involved two women who, during separate sessions went back to a period in 1904 when they reported being dancehall girls in France. They were strangers to each other until I brought them together. Much to the surprise of all of us, they reported that they not only knew each other, but worked at the same dancehall at the same time.

An incident they relived together was related with much hilarity. The girls' living quarters were located on the second floor above the dancehall. One evening after the show, a rejected suitor climbed up and tried to enter the window of their room. With much laughter, they discussed with each other (both were in hypnosis at the time) how they slammed the window on his fingers. Then while laughing so hard they could hardly speak, said, "And the next morning do you know what we found on the window sill? One of his fingers."

The present lives of these two women is quite diverse from the story told and acted out with high believability. However, both are fun-loving and mischievous, and it was not difficult to imagine them in the roles they had described.

These are only a few of the possible ways to gather evidence for the possible uses and benefits of hypnosis. There seems to me to be no limit of what we can explore if we are willing to probe deeply with open minds as to what we will find. Greater profit would undoubtedly follow such probing than could possibly follow the use of our energies arguing as to whether there is anything to probe.

We do not have to argue. We can test, experiment, explore. Such investigation is not only potentially beneficial, but an exciting and satisfying adventure.

Chapter 15

WHAT POSSESSES US?

"If we would guide by the light of reason, we must let our minds be bold."   Justice Brandeis

A fairly commonly used phrase is, "I don't know what possessed me to do that." Another is, "Like one possessed."

Ordinarily these phrases denote brief abberant behavior that is different from the usual or normal behavior of that person. By these phrases, we are not speaking of an actual possession by a spirit or demon.

A valid question is — Is there such a phenomenon as actual possession by another mind, another entity, another being of some kind?

Among my patients were several who appeared to be experiencing actual possession by a different mind and personality than their own. One even manifested seven additional personalities. These could possibly be the so-called dissociated or split-off segments of their own personality. However, after dealing with them first hand, I prefer to accept what they say they are — other personalities using the body temporarily.

None of my patients have manifested the type of "possession" so dramatically depicted in *The Exorcist*. Nor have they shown any of the violent or degrading patterns ordinarily associated with "demon" possession.

One particularly interesting case for me was a young woman who had a two-day gap in her memory. She came to me in the hope that I could help her find out what had happened in the time period between a very hot Sunday afternoon and the following Tuesday evening. She had no memory of events during those two days.

She could consciously recall the family picnic in her back

yard on a very hot Sunday afternoon — then all was blank until she wakened in a hospital bed on Tuesday evening. Although her family told her very little about the non-remembered two days, she felt that they were deliberately withholding information from her. She wanted the two-day gap filled in if possible.

Digging out this information required several sessions with hypnosis before she came to understand what she had done and her reason for doing so.

After several rather unproductive sessions, she suddenly reported that she had attempted to hang herself from the rafters in her garage that Sunday afternoon. She was puzzled about this as she did not recognize in herself any suicidal tendencies. Further probing brought out the statement that she had not done the hanging. She had been possessed by another being who had done it instead. She further stated that she had become possessed on this day because she had in the past possessed a body not her own.

I asked her to tell me about the time she had possessed another body. She went to April 1906, in San Francisco. She was a dance-hall girl named Millie, and was employed at a well known night spot. She died in the great earthquake. Here is an excerpt from one of the tape recordings:

A. S.   Oh, the noise! Um-m-m-m. Oh, God!

Dr. H.   What's happening?

A. S.   I don't know. I don't know. The end of the world. It's the end of the world.

Dr. H.   Tell me what you are talking about.

A. S.   Oh, my God! Oh!

Dr. H.   Now what's happening to you? Where are you? Are you still Milly?

A. S.   I'm lost.

Dr. H.   You're lost? Just look around and describe what you see. (It was later that I realized that she was confused because she had left the body of Milly.)

A. S.   It's fires.

Dr. H.   Fires?

A. S.   Noise—like a roar—and people screaming.

Dr. H.   Can you hear the people screaming?

A. S.   Animals! Oh the animals! The horses and the fire! The whole sky is lit up with the flames.

Dr. H.   Where are you when you can see all this?

A. S.   I don't know, but I can see it.

Dr. H.   Where do you seem to be?

A. S.   (Surprised,) Oh! I'm higher than Nob Hill. And nothing is higher than Nob Hill.

Dr. H.   Is there any particular activity that you notice?

A. S.   Oh, there is so much activity.

Dr. H.   You watch a while and if there is anything which particularly catches your attention, tell me what it is.

A. S.   I think ... I think it is the people trying to get away . . . away from the walls—the walls of flames . . . . to the water.

Dr. H.   What are these people doing?

A. S.   They are at the water's edges . . . the water's edge ... all over the dock ... thousands of them . . . they are moving boats, boats of all kinds—big ones, little ones, ferry boats. Men are pushing women and children away. Oh, it's pandemonium.

Dr. H.   Go on, tell everything you notice.

A. S.   I'm falling asleep.

Dr. H.   Asleep? Where are you?

A. S.   I'm out on a boat.

Dr. H.   How did you get out on the boat?

A. S.   I came aboard.

Dr. H. What is your name?

A. S. Ruth.

Dr. H. A few moments ago you said your name was Milly. Let's go back to the time you were Milly at the Tivoli. The walls began falling down.

A. S. The Tivoli is gone.

Dr. H. Where are you?

A. S. I don't know.

Dr. H. Just give me a review of the events between the time you are at the Tivoli and when you are on the boat.

A. S. There are people—thousands of them getting into boats to leave the wall of flames. So we are on the boat.

Dr. H. How did you get on the boat?

A. S. I got on the boat. (She did not then understand it herself.) I just went ahead and got on the boat.

Dr. H. How did it happen that your name was Milly, and now it's Ruth?

A. S. Well, there was this little girl. I don't know too much about her, but I will. She had a very bad head injury, I guess. The whole head is bandaged, you see. She is with a man and a woman. I don't think they know—I'm sure they don't.

Dr. H. What is it that they don't know?

A. S. That the little girl is dead. Her body was empty, so I went in.

Dr. H. Then what happens?

A. S. I'm the little girl.

Dr. H. How do you do this?

A. S. I don't know how you do it, you just do it.

Dr. H.   When you get into this little girl's body, are you Milly, or do you have a different name?

A. S.   No, the little girl's name is Ruth, so I'm Ruth.

Dr. H.   As Ruth you go across the water, and you are aware of where you are going and when you get there.

A. S.   Well, I am trying to be aware, but I am not aware of anything. All I know is that my head hurts and I want to sleep.

At this point the subject was advanced in time to when her head did not hurt her. This proved to be many months later. She was still convalescing from her injuries and an illness resulting from the earthquake. We continued the advancement until she found herself at age 16, in 1917, at a picnic in Golden Gate Park. She described the picnic and how her boyfriend had some horses which they rode in the park. Finally, the horse she was riding became frightened, bolted and threw her off. She died from the fall.

If what was said here is valid, then my patient, A. S., was once a dance-hall girl named Milly, who died in the 1906 earthquake . . The soul of Milly was able to observe the fire, the animals, the people from a place "higher than Nob Hill." Her attention was drawn to a body of a little girl with a bandaged head. She was aware that the body was empty — her soul had gone — so she went in and possessed the body called Ruth. She lived in that body of Ruth until 1917, when at the age of sixteen, she fell from a horse in Golden Gate Park and died.

After we had filled in the details of the life of Ruth, I asked her to come again to the hot Sunday afternoon on which she had stopped remembering. With a note of astonishment, she was able to fill in that Sunday. She realized that she had become overheated and had passed out. Another personality, hostile and crude, had taken over her unconscious body, had behaved rudely and harshly with her family (completely out of character for her) and had gone into the garage and had hanged herself. She was found and cut down in time, taken to the hospital and wakened there Tuesday evening completely herself again.

She then realized that she had possessed the body of

of Ruth and had therefore qualified herself for possession of her own body by an alien spirit.

Another patient, L. N., was my most interesting case of possession. She was a shy, fearful, introverted mother of six who had great difficulty coping with her life. She reported always feeling tired and having to take frequent naps. It was during some of these "naps" that aberrant behavior patterns were manifest. She was not a proficient housekeeper. However, after some "naps" she would waken to find the house unusually tidy, dinner prepared and the children under control.

She was greatly troubled by these times when she was obviously doing things of which she had no memory. These blackouts would last for a few minutes to several hours. Upon coming out of these periods, she had no memory of what had transpired. She would sometimes return to herself in a place she did not ordinarily frequent and dressed in garments she did not recognize. For even a strong personality, this kind of experience is distressing. For her it was devastating. She had earlier consulted an M.D. Psychiatrist who was interested in multiple personalities, and who had, using hypnosis, elicited seven other personalities—all very different from the personality of L. N.

During my sessions with L. N., I met and talked with these seven beings who seemed to share her body. I could only think of them as being what they claimed to be — separate entities or souls. I confess that I did not at first realize what I was dealing with during my work with L. N. It was a surprise to have her respond as follow: (She was deeply hypnotized)

Dr. H.　Describe how you feel.

L. N.　Resting. I just want to keep on resting.

Dr. H.　Now your subconscious mind can tell you why you need such a great deal of rest—what the reason for it is. Just imagine that you are sitting in a theater and the curtain is about to open. At the count of three the curtain will open and there will be some sort of play going on on the stage. You will see it and will describe everything you see. 1,2,3. The curtain is opening. Tell me what you see on the stage.

L. N.   Trees, a path. . . a fence. . . .(She then described herself sitting by a tree feeling at peace and thinking about writing poetry. The subtle change, the softening of her voice were not at first noticed by me. Then she said her name was Cathy, and that she felt such joy in the beauty of nature that she wanted to write about it. By this time the change in her was obvious. This was not the same woman who had entered my office. This was someone else, a totally different personality.)

L. N.   (As Cathy.) I like to think about poetry. (Pause.) I'm getting so big.

Dr. H.   How big?

L. N.   Big as a room. Bigger. . .and bigger. . .and bigger.

Dr. H.   Why are you getting big?

L. N.   I have to get out of this room.

Dr. H.   Is it your room at home?

L. N.   No. . .my. . .my body. I want to go home.

Dr. H.   Tell me your name.

L. N.   I'm going to sleep again. (Marked change in facial expression.)

Dr. H.   What's happening now?

L. N.   (Now in the personality of Ethel.) She's asleep now. (Laughter.)

Dr. H.   Who is asleep?

L. N.   (As Ethel.) Cathy. She's a fool.

Dr. H.   What does Cathy look like?

L. N.   (As Ethel.) She's real droopy. She wants to sit under a tree and write. She's a real drag.

Dr. H.   Where is Cathy's home?

L. N.　(As Ethel.) Oh, she lives here too, but I just pushed her out.

Dr. H.　You don't like Cathy?

L. N.　(Ethel) She's time consuming. She cries a lot.

Dr. H.　How do you feel when she cries?

L. N.　(Ethel, laughing.) I don't care if she cries.

Dr. H.　Can you tell Cathy to go away?

L. N.　(Ethel) She's gone.

At this point Ethel left and a third personality appeared. She announced her name as Alma. She was outspoken, aggressive—one who took control. She told me how she cleaned up the house, spanked the kids if they needed it, didn't sit around whining. She also claimed that L. N.'s husband liked her best.

Dr. H.　What do you have to tell me in addition?

L. N.　(As Alma.) I didn't like that other doctor.

Dr. H.　Why didn't you like him?

L. N.　(Alma) He said I was a liar. He wouldn't listen to me.

Dr. H.　Where do you live, Alma?

L. N.　(Alma) Oh, I live here also. I've lived here for a long time.

Dr. H.　Wouldn't it be better if you went some other place?

L. N.　(Alma, indignantly.) No! I can't go anywhere else, This is my body too. I can't go now. Some day I'll go. It's about my turn anyway.

Dr. H.　You might be having a lot more fun somewhere else.

L. N.　(Alma) Why does everyone try to make me go away. Why doesn't everybody else go away?

Dr. H.　How long have you been here?

L. N.   (Alma) Twenty five or thirty years. . .since I was ten.

Dr. H.   Where were you as a little girl?

L. N.   (Alma) In Wyoming.

In the voice and manner of Alma, there followed a long description of her life in Wyoming and earlier in Alabama. She talked of her school, and how difficult it was to go to school when the snow was deep. At this point L. N. reappeared—at least the voice of L. N. returned. A little more talk about Wyoming and the session ended.

During the second session with L. N., Alma suddenly reappeared.

Dr. H.   Who are you?

L. N.   (Alma) What do you want me to tell you?

Dr. H.   I want to find out why Lilly is having so much difficulty. . .why she is so unhappy. . .why she has difficulty showing confidence and courage. . .

L. N.   (Alma, interrupting.) Because she worries too much.

Dr. H.   What does she worry about?

L. N.   (Alma) Doing the right thing, and. . .

Dr. H.   Has she reason to worry about doing the right thing? Does she usually do the right thing?

L. N.   (Alma) Yeah. Too much. Be better if she kicked up her heels.

Dr. H.   And do something that is not so right and proper?

L. N.   (Alma) Uh-huh.

Dr. H.   What else should Lilly do?

L. N.   (Alma) She needs to tell them to go to hell. . . right straight to hell.

Dr. H.   Who are some of these people that she should

tell to go to hell?

L. N.   (Alma, laughing) Not me!

Dr. H.   How about Dr. Hickman? Should she tell Dr. Hickman to go to hell?

L. N.   (Alma) Maybe. (Mischievous laughter.) At least she should be able to tell them to go to hell! She shouldn't be so unsure and uncertain. (Disgustedly.) If it's so hard to live, then maybe she should just go away. I can live. Because when things get hard for me, I stop. (Big sigh.) I'm just tired.

Dr. H.   What makes you tired?

L. N.   (Alma) Holding everybody down. Mostly her, I guess.

During the conversation that followed I pointed out to Alma that she was trespassing, and that if she wanted a body to use there was a better way of getting one. This brought an emphatic, "But I don't want to be a *baby*."

In other sessions a number of other personalities appeared and spoke through the body of the hypnotized L. N. Seven in all I counted. Each was easily identified as they appeared, having different voice qualities and different personality traits.

L. N. was a most responsive subject. She told me while hypnotized that just before each blackout she would become aware of a very tired feeling and would stop for a rest. I asked her subconscious mind what she needed to meet her blackout problem. She responded that she needed to avoid these drowsy, sleepy periods.

I gave her the suggestion that when she started to feel tired all she needed to do was to sit down and use a hand signal to trigger a burst of energy so that the tired feeling would disappear.

As I gave the suggestion the first time, the voice of Alma burst in interrupting, "You can't do that! Then we couldn't do anything!" Again I tried to explain to her how she could acquire a body of her own, and not need to share it with the others. She almost shouted this time repeating, "But I don't want to be a BABY!"

Whether these other personalities that spoke through L. N. were dissociated parts of herself, or whether they were what they claimed to be—disembodied entities who came in and used L. N.'s body from time to time, did not concern me. I accepted them for what they said they were. In so doing, I had no difficulty dealing with them and in using them to help the patient solve her problems. She gradually learned to control the blackouts.

It seems to me that it is much easier and more logical to accept this phenomenon as what it claims to be rather than try to explain it away by postulating influences with no more basis than theory.

The story of Billy Milligan, told by Author Daniel Keyes includes a reference to the work of Dr. Frank W. Putnam, Jr., a psychiatrist at the National Institute of Health who has tested several multiple personality subjects. Dr. Putnam found that the several personalities also manifested different galvanic skin responses and different brain wave patterns. This strongly suggests that there are actually different souls inhabiting the body at different times, and that manifestation is not due to the splitting of the core personality.

A thorough investigation, using hypnosis would answer these unanswered questions.

Chapter 16

TREATING SEX PROBLEMS

"Sex—The name given to that which was to be God's miracle, but which man hath made a nag which he rideth and hath no destination."

Patience Worth.

Since the days of Sigmund Freud, sexual problems have been held to be the principal causes of neuroses. In my practice, this did not hold true. The percentage of my patients requesting help with sex problems was very small.

The 1780 story told in the early chapters did have a large sexual component, but that was not the complaint that brought her to me. Instead it was her fear, amounting to panic for which she asked help. Among the patients who had specific sex problems were Lisa Beaman, and Diane Moore, (both fictional names) whose cases are discussed later.

However, even for these women, the problem went far beyond sex to encompass other aspects of the self. Only by dealing with the whole person did I feel that I was truly doing them a service worthy of my profession, and the kind of service they had the right to expect.

Lisa Beaman, nearing forty, had numerous sexual complaints. She had had a dismal failure of a marriage. She felt terribly guilty both because of her intermittant promiscuity and her habit of frequent masturbation. She had taken her complaint to several other doctors. One she had seen shortly before coming to me had triggered an exacerbation of her guilt.

This is a partial transcript of one of her hypnosis sessions.

L. B.   Well, these thoughts start following me after this doctor gave me this examination. I don't know what the examination was for, but he moved his finger back and forth in my vagina.

Dr. H.   What was your reason for consulting him? For what complaint?

L. B.   Guess he wasn't looking for anything. He was curious to see if he could arouse me. That's what he was seeing. I felt quite ashamed at the time. I was humiliated and held myself very rigid. I showed nothing, but I wanted to. I wanted to. You see, I have always had the feeling that it wasn't nice and it wasn't right. I knew something was wrong, that I shouldn't feel that way because I was a Christian. I always was very sorry afterwards, after I felt that way. I always asked God to forgive me.

Dr. H.   Did asking God help you?

L. B.   Yes, it helped me. Oh, I felt terribly guilty. I asked God to forgive me. I told God I would never do it again (Referring to masturbation.) One day I found I had made a terrible mistake because I found I had no control over that. It kept coming and coming . . . there it would be and it would frighten me. I was afraid that God would strike me dead, simply because I went back on my vow. I did it again, but God didn't strike me dead. God didn't do anything to me. I shouldn't have made the vow. I'll never make another vow as long as I live. I couldn't keep my vow. (Crying.) I couldn't. I was afraid. I was terrified. I knew God would punish me for making a vow I couldn't keep. I didn't know when I made it that I couldn't keep it. I thought I was doing something terrible. I thought it was so terrible wrong because everybody hid—everybody was so secretive about how they have babies and what they did to have babies. They'd whisper it and nobody would tell me. They acted like it was something evil. I didn't know when two people come together like that, having intercourse. I didn't know that's how they had babies anyway. I didn't know what happened. I just thought that that was nasty, it was just not nice, and it was something that was a dark deep secret ... Yes, get diseases too. Terrible things they do. Red light districts where they go. I was gonna go see one. I always wanted to see what a red light district looked like. It's always been a great mystery to me. Somebody said "a whore house." I finally found out it meant the same thing. An awful part of town! Oh God! They'd go to hell. If I did those things I'd go to hell. Terrible, horrible. To go to such places. To go to such places, oh! Here . . . . . Oh my goodness. . . . here I have the same kind of a feeling.

Dr. H.   Go on — talk about your feelings.

L. B.   Here I've got the same kind of a feeling. Maybe it wasn't so bad as it was shown to me. At night everybody feels like that and if they don't have someone ... I mean if they're not married or if they don't have a good relationship ... well it seems like, goodness sakes, they got to do something. They had harlots in Bible days. God didn't send them to hell because of that. I don't think anybody would go to hell because of that.

Dr. H.   Is you fear all gone now?

L. B.   What fear?

Dr. H.   You said you were afraid of those feelings.

L. B.   I don't have any fear now. I wouldn't blame any man for going to a harlot if he had no other way.

Dr. H.   Does this apply to both men and women?

L. B.   Yeah. Man or woman. What are they gonna do? After all, look at me. At night you could always straighten yourself out for a while. How else they gonna learn. Oh sure. It's a mistake, a pitiful mistake because there is a life, another life. Yes, a pitiful mistake. Somebody failed when it goes that far. It doesn't have to go that far. It isn't bad, but it isn't right either.

Dr. H.   Why do you say it isn't right?

L. B.   It isn't right because God has given us a plan. There is a right way, a relationship that God has given us . . . . to marry. That's the right path for us to take. We do get off the beaten path and that's what causes the other things to be. People have failed — mothers and fathers have failed — if the young people had the right relationship with mother and father these things wouldn't happen. They may be tempted, but it wouldn't happen because they'll realize that it will be a beautiful thing, and its something worth waiting for.

Dr. H.   Are you now more comfortable with your feelings?

L. B.   Well, I have sex feelings.

Dr. H.   Does this bother you?

L. B.   Well, I've always fought it.

Dr. H.   Are you going to be able to stop fighting it?

L. B.   Well, how do I stop fighting it? I don't think it is wrong. God made us that way, but what you have to learn is how to control it within your own self. Each one has got to learn how to control this emotion. That's what's the matter with me. I've let it run away with me all my life. It's a creative emotion. I realize that. It's a creative act, but how do I handle it? It's there. I can't deny it, and it's very strong, very powerful emotion. I can't just shut it off.

Dr. H.   What can you do about it?

L. B.   I have to accept it. Have to learn to live with it. It seems like the wall I have built around myself is getting smaller. In a dream I threw up my

> legs and looked at that man sitting over there seeing me. I was ashamed because I knew he was seeing me.

Dr. H.   What is wrong with that?

L. B.   He didn't see anything new. I haven't got anything to hide and be ashamed of. The reason I was ashamed of what I had to show was because I feel that way, like I've got something to hide and I'm ashamed. I wouldn't have felt, have had such strong feelings about somebody seeing me if I . . . huh! I haven't got anything to hide. I didn't know it. I thought I had something to hide. It's no secret. Everybody knows what it's like anyway. Oh, I didn't know it!

Dr. H.   Are you feeling better now?

L. B.   Oh yes! But I still have more learning to do.

One of my most satisfying cases was another who came to me with the problem of inability to form a really satisfactory relationship with any man. She realized that something within herself was the hindrance, but she was only vaguely aware of what should be done to correct the flaw within herself. She was placed in a state of hypnosis and instructed to find and report the cause of her problem.

D. M.   It is because I don't give of myself. I always sort of hunch over and go in sideways to a place where I can take all of the good out of a man without ever having to expose myself enough to give.

Dr. H.   Do I understand you to say that you have the urge to get more than you give?

D. M.   Yes, that's what I want. I want to be able to give.

Dr. H.   What does you subconscious have to say about your inability to give?

D. M.   It ruins everything.

Dr. H.   Does is ruin just marriage, or other things too?

D. M.   Everything. Every situation.

Dr. H.   Is your subconscious telling you that you must change this wanting to get more than you give?

D. M.   I've got to be able to give without any concern as to whether I get or not.

Dr. H.   That's good advice. Has your subconscious anything else to say about the problems you have mentioned?

D. M.   It's just that if I would become involved ... if I really accept this a lot of the pain goes away too. It doesn't hurt to give, if you're really giving.

Dr. H.   Then your subconscious says it would be easier and less painful if you were to start giving more? Is that right?

D. M.   Yes.

Dr. H.   Would it be nice to have a life that was less painful?

D. M.   Yes.

Dr. H.   Are you ready to begin this now?

D. M.   I've been ready for a long time, but I wouldn't.

Dr. H.   Are there really any major flaws in your personality or your attitude?

D. M.   Just this selfishness. That's the only thing that is ever wrong with anybody. We're all doing it.

Dr. H.   Is that the reason you are here?

D. M.   Yes. We have to keep coming back until it gets all drained out of us. It is so easy to play games and tell yourself you don't do this. The results are still the same. It isn't any good.

Dr. H.   When we get tired of hurting what happens?

D. M.   We have to find some other way to do it. But

what makes you really learn it so that you do more than just talk about it?

Dr. H.   Is it when you hurt enough?

D. M.   It's like you have to have reminders all the time. It's a hard thing!

Dr. H.   If you were able to give, could you then expect that others might also give to you?

D. M.   Yes. Then I wouldn't have to be so concerned about whatever it is that I have held so close. But there is still one little part of me though that wants to stay hidden away.

Dr. H.   What is it?

D. M.   There's one little thing that I have to protect. One little tiny thing that ... it's almost like carrying a baby, and you feel that your whole body is concerned with protecting the baby. It's like a little seed that still has to be protected because we just aren't ready to let go of it.

Dr. H.   As you are growing are you coming to the place where you will be ready to let go of it?

D. M.   Yes. When I let all the rest go, this will have room to grow and then it can go. If only I keep growing—stop playing around, stop playing games. I have to just relax and let things happen, and be aware of what's happening. This is why it has always been so hard to be really passive ..... because I had the belief that being passive and being stupid was the same thing.

Dr. H.   Whom have you known who was passive and stupid?

D. M.   My brother!

Dr. H.   Is it always necessary to be stupid to be passive?

D. M.   No. That's what I just now know!

Dr. H.   Do you also need to learn more patience?

D. M.   Yes. Because I can do anything for a little while, but if I don't get results immediately I just give it up. I don't stay with it. I don't give myself a chance. Maybe you get even more awareness when you're passive . . . stop fighting the whole world, then your mind is free to see a lot of things. But now when I start fighting I'll know what I'm doing. It's not something I'm going to give up. I sort of feel that I've just set up little checks for myself, and when I start off on the old kick there will be a little prod back in the right direction and that's good . . . like a signpost . . . . enough so that I will know when I'm off the track.

Dr. H.   Does your subconscious have anything to say about this question of being feminine or being masculine?

D. M.   Really I am feminine, but I'm afraid to admit it. I feel like . . . almost like a little kitten that really can't do things, but again there is the fear of being stepped on or something . . . just being worthless.

Dr. H.   If a woman is passive, does that mean she is any less feminine?

D. M.   No, because then she doesn't have to be concerned with all the outside things. It's better the men have to worry about everything else. There's a softness that feels so good. It's just nice to love and not demand response. It's only the demanding part of loving that ever hurts. It's like suddenly you see a letter that explains everything, and you realize it's been there all the time. I used to look for a man who had a lot of the feminine because I thought this would complete what I thought I lacked. Just to *be*, to exist, to breathe and move, to quit fighting, and grabbing, and pulling. *It seems so simple I'm irritated!*

Dr. H.   How could you have missed it so long?

D. M.   That's just it. There doesn't seem to be any reason.

Dr. H.   What is the reason? Let us go back to the time . . . . the first time when something happened that made you feel that it was better to be more masculine than feminine. What was it? Tell what happened.

D. M.   There was a real good time when I was a man.

Dr. H.   Tell me all about it.

D. M.   It wasn't very long, but just good feelings, all the fun of growing up and being able to go off with the boys and men and all the women had to stay home. It felt so good. I could do things, outside things. It was sort of like being an animal, but I was contented that way. I was strong and it felt good.

Dr. H.   Did you sense the lack?

D. M.   Not then. I thought that was all there was to life. It was good. To be a woman then was an awful thing. It was better to be a man. You were free and you could do things. Now all the bad feelings I have about myself are feelings I had then about all women, that they really aren't worth much. But I didn't know *anything* then! There just wasn't any inside feeling. If I could have gotten that then, I would have begun to know a little bit more. It's almost like the whole lifetime was just wasted . . . a blank page . . . just a big recess. Yet it was real good.

Dr. H.   Did you learn that men must have some feminine qualities?

D. M.   Yes, they have to be whole—to be something more than a strapping young buck.

Dr. H.   Does a woman also have to have some of the masculine qualities to be whole?

D. M.   A good woman does.

Dr. H.   Do you have enough of these masculine qualities?

D. M.   Yes. Those I have enough of. The whole trouble is in trying to enlarge those so terrifically to cover up the bad feeling about being a woman. I'm awfully glad I'm a woman, really. Because women can use both qualities a lot better. It's hard for a man to use both. A lot of things women are expected to do take courage and strength and planning and everything . . . just like men. But they can be all as soft as they want to at the same time.

Dr. H.   What happens if the man is soft?

D. M.   Then people don't accept it as easily. Because — you know women have soft of . . . part of the idea of getting control of the man was to make them play down this very thing that was important to them . . . It's not other men that would ridicule the softness. A woman can respond to it in one male. Oh this is all mixed up. A woman can respond real easily to softness in her particular male, but she has to sort of give the impression that she expects men in general not to be so soft and gentle and everything . . . that boy, if they are going out and going to meet the world, that they have to be tough and that sort of thing, and it undermines them . . . it takes away their most strength really. It's a foolish thing to have done. If you let the man have the feminine qualities then he can be content and doesn't need as much from you. He is more complete within himself . . . then he can relate without having to deprive you of any part of yourself. If a woman really feels complete then it is no threat to her to see the softness in a man. She can let him have this softness . . . let it temper his masculinity. Gee, if everyone were all whole it would be just fine.

Dr. H.   You have done very well. Is there anything else

you need to say or is this enough for today?

D. M.   This is enough.

These two cases were selected as examples of the possibilities inherent in the use of hypnosis as a tool for exploring the unconscious. These two girls represent wide divergence of background and adjustment to life. They possessed different qualities of intelligence, different educational experiences, different attitudes toward religion and different responses to the social mores. In spite of this wide divergence on the conscious mind level, the responses of both of them showed a common ability to understand their own sexuality. Each also added comments of value in building a philosophical structure on which to base future choices.

Lisa Beaman was my patient for over a year. I was able to observe her progress in integrating the insights evoked in this and other sessions into her life pattern. Although there was still much need for growth when our relationship ended, she had lost her great fear of life, her guilt regarding her body, and her inability to function in society.

I saw Diane Moore only once for a colleague, a psychologist who was vacationing. He later informed me that she was successfully utilizing the experiences and insights from this one session with me in developing further self-understanding.

Even after years of working with hypnosis, I am frequently surprised at the rapidity with which some patients can probe their inner nature and gain understanding of themselves. Neither of these girls was consciously aware of the causes of their problems before the hypnotic sessions, yet both were able to describe both the causative factors and the changes that were desirable for themselves. In addition both were able to produce valuable material of a philosophical nature.

My work with hypnosis indicates that each of our unconscious minds can be likened to vast unexplored continents, containing both adventures and treasures beyond our greatest expectations. I think of hypnosis as a tool that will help us to tap these unexplored levels of our minds, the vast storehouse of knowledge and wisdom that has been tapped to so small a degree. My work with hypnosis has also added substance to the concept of a racial unconscious as postulated by the late Dr. Carl G. Jung.

Another thing that my patients have taught me is that we may very widely at a conscious level and remain in agreement when functioning from a deeper level.

If hypnosis truly is such a tool, then it should be more and more widely used. If its value is small or non-existent, as some authorities claim, this too should be known and demonstrated by research and controlled experimentation. The words of authorities expressing conflicting opinions is not enough.

If man's nature is, as my cases have indicated it to be, that of an immortal soul living in a series of physical bodies, acquiring learning that is carried from one life to the next, continuing to evolve according to a great creative plan, and finally uniting with the Universal Creative Spirit or God, then this too should be a part of our body of knowledge.

EPILOGUE

"I adopted the theory of Reincarnation when I was twenty-six ... Religion offered nothing to that point ... Even work could not give me complete satisfaction. Work is futile if we cannot utilize the experience we collect in one life in the next. When I discovered Reincarnation it was as if I had found a universal plan. Time no longer limited. I was no longer slave to the hands of the clock ... Genius is experience. Some seem to think that it is a gift or talent, but it is the fruit of long experience in many lives ...

The discovery of Reincarnation put my mind at ease ... If you preserve a record of this conversation write it so that it puts men's minds at ease. I would like to communicate to others the calmness that the long view of life gives to us."

Henry Ford—Interview,
S.F. Examiner, August 1928

The cases presented in this book illustrate how ghosts from the past persist in affecting our behavior. Ghosts from far distant past may be as potent an effect as ghosts from the childhood years of our present life.

We persist in reacting automatically not to situations as they truly exist, but to the past, childishly feeling resentment, anger or fear where none is appropriate. These feelings can sometimes find expression in physical symptoms or physiological malfunction. The body finds a way to manifest pent-up feelings and release them. Sometimes the feelings are released by aberrant behavior patterns, conflict with other people or even true mental illness.

The demands of a situation cannot be clearly perceived through the clouds of childish habit patterns from the past, clouds of fears, hates, anxieties, pride, lonliness or frustrations. It is only when these clouds have been penetrated, explored and dispelled that we can become free to trust our feelings and our intellect as guides to conduct—free to develop our capacities as thinking, feeling persons acting in harmony, and free from the rigid codes we have so long used as substitutes for this harmony. Conformity at all cost can give way to true recognition of the source of behavior patterns, and to the legitimate and socially acceptable outlet for feelings of hostility and agression.

If these ghosts had their origin in former life experiences in other bodies, then they must be sought out at their point of origin. The emotional price-tag of failure to do this is far too high — not only for the individual but for the nation — even for the whole human race.

The end